LATINA WRITERS

THE ILAN STAVANS LIBRARY OF LATINO CIVILIZATION

LATINA WRITERS

Edited by Ilan Stavans

GREENWOOD PRESS
Westport, Connecticut • London

Library of Congress Cataloging-in-Publication Data

Latina writers / Ilan Stavans, editor.
      p. cm. — (The Ilan Stavans library of Latino civilization, ISSN 1938–615X)
  Includes bibliographical references and index.
  ISBN-13: 978–0–313–34806–8 (alk. paper)
  1. American literature—Hispanic American authors—History and criticism.
2. American literature—Women authors—History and criticism.   3. American
literature—20th century—History and criticism.   4. American literature—
21st century—History and criticism.   5. Hispanic Americans in literature.
6. Hispanic American women authors—Political and social views.   7. Feminism and
literature.   8. Homosexuality and literature.   I. Stavans, Ilan.
  PS153.H56L37   2008
  810.9'9287'08968—dc22   2008007879

British Library Cataloguing in Publication Data is available.

Library of Congress Catalog Card Number: 2008007879
ISBN: 978–0–313–34806–8
ISSN: 1938–615X

First published in 2008

Greenwood Press, 88 Post Road West, Westport, CT 06881
An imprint of Greenwood Publishing Group, Inc.
www.greenwood.com

Printed in the United States of America

The paper used in this book complies with the
Permanent Paper Standard issued by the National
Information Standards Organization (Z39.48–1984).

10 9 8 7 6 5 4 3 2 1

Contents

SERIES FOREWORD

The book series The Ilan Stavans Library of Latino Civilization, the first of its kind, is devoted to exploring all the facets of Hispanic civilization in the United States, with its ramifications in the Americas, the Caribbean Basin, and the Iberian Peninsula. The objective is to showcase its richness and complexity from a myriad perspective. According to the U.S. Census Bureau, the Latino minority is the largest in the nation. It is also the fifth largest concentration of Hispanics in the globe.

Out of every seven Americans, one traces his or her roots to the Spanish-speaking world. Mexicans make up about 65 percent of the minority. Other major national groups are Puerto Ricans, Cubans, Dominicans, Ecuadorians, Guatemalans, Nicaraguans, Salvadorans, and Colombians. They are either immigrants, descendants of immigrants, or dwellers in a territory (Puerto Rico, the Southwest) having a conflicted relationship with the mainland United States. As such, they are the perfect example of *encuentro:* an encounter with different social and political modes, an encounter with a new language, an encounter with a different way of dreaming.

The series is a response to the limited resources available and the abundance of stereotypes, which are a sign of lazy thinking. The twentieth-century Spanish philosopher José Ortega y Gasset, author of *The Revolt of the Masses,* once said: "By speaking, by thinking, we undertake to clarify things, and that forces us to exacerbate them, dislocate them, schematize them. Every concept is in itself an exaggeration." The purpose of the series is not to clarify but to complicate our understanding of Latinos. Do so many individuals from different national, geographic, economic, religious, and ethnic backgrounds coalesce as an integrated whole? Is there an *unum* in the *pluribus*?

Baruch Spinoza believed that everything in the universe wants to be preserved in its present form: a tree wants to be a tree, and a dog a dog. Latinos in the United States want to be Latinos in the United States—no easy task, and therefore an intriguing one to explore. Each volume of the series contains an assortment of approximately a dozen articles, essays, and interviews never gathered together before. The authors are scholars, writers, journalists, and specialists in their respective fields. The selection is followed by a bibliography of important resources. The compilation is designed to generate debate and foster research: to complicate our knowledge. Every attempt is made to balance the ideological viewpoint of the authors. The target audience is students, specialists, and the lay reader. Thematically, the volumes will range from politics to sports, from music to cuisine. Historical periods and benchmarks such as the Mexican War, the Spanish-American War, the Zoot Suit Riots, the Bracero Program, and the Cuban Revolution, as well as controversial topics such as immigration, bilingual education, and Spanglish, will be tackled.

Democracy is only able to thrive when it engages in an open, honest transaction of information. By offering diverse, insightful collections of provocative, informed, insightful material about Hispanic life in the United States and inviting people to engage in critical thinking, The Ilan Stavans Library of Latino Civilization seeks to offer critical tools that open new vistas to appreciate the fastest growing, increasingly heterogeneous minority in the nation—to be part of the *encuentro*.

Ilan Stavans

PREFACE

Although Latinos have been an essential component of U.S. history even before the nation became independent, only in recent years has their literature been embraced by a wide selection of readers. This boom, in part, is the result of the demographic transformation of the country as a whole, and, obviously, of the rapid growth of the Hispanic minority itself, which, according to the Census Bureau, is the largest since 2003.

Arguably the most extraordinary feature in this boom is the fact that Latina writers are firmly at the helm. Hispanic women have been writing about their experience in America, autobiographically and in poetic and fictional terms, since the nineteenth century. Prior to that period, society was clearly dominated by men. The female voices available at the time are mostly of nuns and other religious devotees whose diaries chronicle their commitment to Jesus Christ. It was only after the Mexican-American War that figures such as Eulalia Pérez, María Amparo Ruíz de Burton, Lola Rodríguez de Tió, Leonor Villegas de Magnón, Adelina "Nina" Otero Warren, and Cleofas Jaramillo found the space to discuss their viewpoints. Their successors, María Cristina Mena, Fabiola Cabeza de Baca Gilbert, Jovita González de Mireles, Julia de Burgos, and Josephina Niggli, opened up the cannon even further.

The national diversity among Latinas is enthralling. Julia Alvarez chronicles in novels such as *How the Garcia Girls Lost Their Accents* the struggle of immigrant women from the Dominican Republic; Cristina García, in her generational saga, *Dreaming in Cuban,* ponders the tension between mothers and daughters as a result of Fidel Castro's revolution in 1958–1959; and Denise Chávez, in her plays and fiction (such as *The Last of the Menu Girls* to *Loving Pedro Infante*), examines the intersection of pop culture and identity among *nuevomexicanas*.

This volume offers a gamut of essays on and by Latina writers from a variety of theoretical perspectives including feminism, postmodernism, postcolonialism, historicism, subaltern, diaspora, gender, border, linguistic, and pan-American studies. It also features a section of *testimonios*, that is, first-hand accounts (at times in the form of personal essays, others via interviews) by novelists, playwrights, memoirists, poets, and activists. The eclecticism of the viewpoints is the message. Phillipa Kafka starts by mapping the cultural landscape of Latina literature. Debra A. Castillo offers a panoramic perspective of Chicana criticism. Jacqueline Zeff looks at the female body. Jacqueline Stefanko focuses on the fragmentation—in individuals, families, and communities—that comes with exile and nostalgia. And Ian Barnard reflects on Gloria Anzaldúa's reformulation of the concept of *mestizaje* through queer theory. Judith Ortiz Cofer and Esmeralda Santiago reflect on their Puerto Ricanness from a personal viewpoint while Sherezada "Chiqui" Vicioso, María Irene Fornés, and Cherríe L. Moraga analyze the crossroads where gender, politics, and literature meet. I've also included a polemical piece of mine on Sandra Cisneros, the best-selling author of *The House on Mango Street*.

Attempting to square these divergent views in between covers isn't my objective. Nor do I want to look at this literary phenomenon in facile terms. To read with acumen, one needs to look at things in context, to be informed but also critical. Sandra Cisneros once said that the reason she decided to become a writer is because she could never find novels about her own identity as a Latina. It appears to me that thanks to her and other *hispanas* the young generation is being better served.

PART I
APPRECIATIONS

Saddling La Gringa: Major Themes in the Works of Latina Writers

Phillipa Kafka

Latina writers focus on what Juan Bruce-Novoa calls "profound links between the exile and/or immigrant experience and that of females in a patriarchal society in which they often exist as foreigners or disenfranchised residents" (1989, 81) and what I call "enforced psychic tourism." Yamila Azize Vargas goes even further in her claims for the influence of the immigrant experience in her analysis of the poetry of Carmen Valle, Sandra M. Esteves, and Luz María Umpierre. She believes that their experience of emigration served as "the catalytic agent" for more than their "radicalism and originality," their "feminine and feminist perspective" and "consciousness" (1989, 163). It may also have forced these Latina poets to experience and react to a racist and discriminatory culture with a literature that consciously defended their own culture, its traditions and history, and their "national identity" (1989, 163). For these reasons, how women characters are represented by Latinas in their works is more than the result of any individual Latina author's abiding sense of "enforced psychic tourism": being forced to be other in an alien culture and triply alien and alienated because of gender and race. Latina writers are also aware of being a part of a much larger "discursive setting" (Kutzinski 1993, 213), a system of inequitable power relations of all kinds as a source for multitudes of voluntary and enforced migrations globally.

Once Latina feminist writers grow conscious of enforced alienation, they seek to upset the perpetuation of a traditional "feminine world," both in their own native culture and in the colonizing culture. They begin to envision a different world "founded on a counterculture of feminist and Latin American affirmation." As becomes evident in the works I analyze in this text, some of the key elements of their writing follow from those visions of how it might be for women. These dream visions lead to their espousal of "nontraditional" forms of "love" for women, of the "necessity of a militant struggle" both against patriarchal Latino and Anglo cultures, of a "sacrilegious" attitude toward the Catholic religion, and of a feminist "reinvention of children's tales" (Vargas 1989, 163). Through revisioning "the plots of patriarchal culture" in a variety of ways, Latina writers are making concerted efforts, not so much to recover their psychic "wholeness" (López Springfield 1994, 701), as in the hope of accelerating movement into new ways, into a new world.

Regardless of their own original class origins, Latina writers tend to depict oppressed working-class female characters, their experiences of daily life, and their realities "from the perspective of the oppressed classes: workers, peasants, women" (Vélez 1988, 4). Horno-Delgado et al. take this argument one step further. They advise readers to view Latina writers' work from a working-class perspective in many ways: "racial, economic, ethnic, political, social, chronological, culinary, ideological, luminous, and stylistic," as "a springboard" in terms of "cultural context" for any "analysis of Latin American literature" (1989a, 12) readers would hope to make.

Within this lower class context, Latina writers tend to focus on women's lives, on how it is like to live "within a woman's space." They generally depict an all-female family, both to reflect reality and to accomplish this goal. Further, many Latinas are themselves from immigrant or exile families. Migration frequently wreaks havoc on the traditional family organization in Hispanic culture. Authors reflecting their own experience, displace the typical "central patriarchal figure" and, instead, depict "a woman-headed and woman-populated household" (Horno-Delgado et al., 1989a, 12), as in Judith Ortiz Cofer's *Silent Dancing* and Magali García Ramis's *Happy Days, Uncle Sergio*. They are not reflecting their visions for a new-world order, only reality as they know it, because they still show traditional patriarchal family models being followed. This is despite the weakness and/or absence of the patriarch, as readers will observe in my analysis of both texts. I analyze this phenomenon from the context of inequitable gendered power relations as perpetuated and mediated by the family's female gatekeepers.

Horno-Delgado et al. also argue that inequitable gendered power relations as a topic for analysis is ignored and subsumed by traditional culture carriers such as gatekeepers whose perception of diversity is only racial or ethnic. Such a limited perspective perpetuates the "division, oppression, inequality, and internalized inferiority of women [of color], especially in contemporary capitalism" (1989a, 13). Again, it is my contention that although I agree that gatekeepers think and act in total obedience to women's relationship to the "power structures" within Latino culture, they do so in all other cultures as well, regardless of whether the culture is capitalist, or fascist, or communist.

The family setup, as buttressed by religious and secular law, as well as social customs that evolve from them, is the single most critiqued institution in the works of Latina writers. But the family is not the cause of women's problems—inequitable gendered power relations are. As Judith Resnik astutely perceives, "power and subordination—not families—are the place from which to begin." Latina writers view "women's oppression" by men in their cultures as emanating not from the family per se, but from how the family is organized so that "men's dominance is constructed and maintained." To reinforce the restrictions on women in the home, all other institutions outside the home practice and maintain male domination, and in all those institutions "women's conceptual location" is situated basically within the structure of "family life" (Resnik 1996, 965).

Is it any wonder then that in describing and analyzing inequitable gendered power relations between men and women, Latina writers, instead of "sanitizing" their feminine psyches often use violent imagery? Their purpose in doing so not only is to forge in a creative way, through writing, a sense of healthy self-identity in the face of a culture that militates against it. As Janice Haaken puts it:

> There is a liberatory aspect to the implicit recognition . . . that feminine spaces are often receptacles for male conflict. Men often do act out their own frustrated longings and displaced rage through women. The feminine recovery of a sense of goodness and entitlement inevitably involves reprojecting the "bad" luck onto the oppressor. But if all discordant and powerful feelings must be projected back onto the oppressor, it leaves women with no space for the integration of unsettling feelings or destructive impulses into a positive sense of self. (1996, 1086)

For Latina writers, as for feminists everywhere, the act of writing to vent their rage against oppression fills the receptive space that is too often lacking outside of the individual woman. However, I would add to Haaken's observations that beyond merely expressing their own subjectivity fully, especially their outrage against inequitable gendered power relations, Latina writers also wish to serve their community, their society, and their world in an ongoing effort to improve it.

All critics of Latina literature are united in emphasizing that it most frequently confronts "sexual inequality in both Anglo and Latino cultures," as well as racism. Interestingly, the writers I have studied emphasize class issues as well, viewing class as one of the key components in their analysis, with gender and race issues within that paradigm. Horno-Delgado et al.'s analysis of Latina writers in this regard serves as a typical example of the failure by critics to recognize the inclusion of class issues in Latina works, let alone an emphasis on them. They perceive Latina writers as engaged in a struggle to effect social and political change with their primary focus on the need for equality for all, especially equality for women. Activism is necessary to achieve this. Simultaneously Latina writers confront racism in the Anglo culture attitude toward Latinos.

Latina writers also rage "against the double standard." Because they live in a situation where they have to deal with "several oppressions simultaneously," they seek to break the barrier of culturally ordained silence. Periodically expressing themselves through angry venting is characteristic of their writing (Horno-Delgado et al. 1989a, 15–17). I contend that Latina writers not only show anger at the oppressions of racism and sexism in their works, they also show anger at the oppression of "differential class rankings" in their culture and between men and women.

Nancy Saporta Sternbach and others have contended rightly that Latina anger about sexism and their priority of interest about all its manifestations, including the suppression of female sexual subjectivity, is not always seen as a priority for women of color as it is for white feminists. Sternbach and others contend that it is only a priority for white feminists, not Latinas. Sexism is viewed by Latina writers "concurrently with other issues such as class, ethnicity, cultural norms, traditions, and the paramount position of the family." So "simplistic" (that is, selfish) are white feminists that they have not even "begun to perceive the complexities of being a Latina woman in the United States, let alone a Latina feminist." As a result, "difficult lessons for white women" (1989, 51) have to be learned by them. The argument that issues relating to sexism are not Latina priorities, but that white feminists only concern themselves with sexism and are not concerned with "other issues" such as "class, ethnicity," and so on is specious. The fact is that these issues are now being "viewed concurrently" by most feminists—white, ethnic, and of color. It would appear that Sternbach is essentializing white feminists when she divides feminists along racial lines. She is, in fact, guilty of what she is accusing white feminists, by taking only one aspect of their agenda into account and not any other issues that they focus on "concurrently." In fact, Latina and white feminist writers' perspectives are similar, far more so than she would grant. Rosario Ferré states the prevailing Latina perspective succinctly and allegorically in "The Bitches' Colloquy": "His misogyny takes my bark away" (1994, 895). That is, the patriarchy silences women. I submit that the primary motive for most Latina writing, as of most white feminist writing, is the attempt through writing to overcome the impossibility "of speaking within dominant discourses without being imprisoned by silencing codes and repressive institutions" (Scorczewski 1996, 320). In this text, I explore how Latina writers depict female gatekeepers as mediators, as wardens, who assist in imprisoning their young charges in the patriarchal institutions of Latino and Anglo cultures.

It is a mistake, as I have argued elsewhere, for groups of women in any and all cultures to separate and distance from each other. We should not continue to be divided and conquered everywhere. We should expand our perspectives to become ever more global. We should emphasize commonalities, regardless of divisions along lines of privilege, or apparent privilege, because as Janice Dewey sees it, "Overshadowed by dominant, partial, and repressive cultural values, all women, women of color, lesbians, are displaced and marginalized" (1989, 46).

The Latina writers are also creating new genres "between poetry and fiction, blurring the line between the short story and the novel, between conversation and literary discourse" (Horno-Delgado et al. 1989a, 17). Judith Ortiz Cofer's *Silent Dancing* serves well as the model in this regard, as readers will discover.

Other Latina writers, such as Rosario Ferré also revise legends and myths and traditional children's tales. Kisenija Bilbija, writing about "The Youngest Doll," states that in the way she writes this tale Ferré thereby situates "a feminist translation of the golem fable into a socio-political space resonant with the United States–Puerto Rico relationship" (1994, 887). Readers will also see Cofer taking the same political stance toward the United States in her myth about Maria Sabida, as does Ramis, as well, in *Happy Days, Uncle Sergio*, through her narrator Lidia and in her haunting characterization of Uncle Sergio. However, Ramis is primarily commited to documenting her characters' lives from a feminist perspective and valorizing and preserving Puerto Rican history and culture.

Latina authors depict many of their female characters exposed to a second batch of success models for women in the United States, in addition to Latino models. Through female gatekeepers, Latino cultures train younger females to reproduce the ways in which they are trained to link their sense of "self-worth" and "self-esteem" to the home and domesticity (de la Torre and Pesquera 1993, 10). Anglo culture only reinforces this training, as Alba Rivera-Ramos puts it, through assigning "the WASPM model as a symbol of superiority." By this means, "any person or group that deviates from this standard is not only different but inferior" (1995, 205). In both their cultures of origin and Anglo culture, gatekeepers work ceaselessly to inscribe into their young female charges notions of female "difference and inferiority." Their goal is to reinforce female obedience to their cultures' construction of discriminatory models for them as ideal women.

Readers will also note an ambivalent quality in Latina writers, despite the fact that they resist both their original and second cultural training and in this sense are "enforced psychic tourists" in two alien cultures. Their resistance is linked to their feminist perspective, but it also includes alert, fully conscious choices to reject as well as to accept certain ideologies from the country of origin and the United States. They make their selections and rejections from a distance, as an observing witness from afar and yet newly, just as a tourist observes an alien culture. Stuart Hall and Donald James define "ideologies" as "concepts, ideas, and images which provide frameworks of interpretation and meaning for social and political thought" (1985, 36). These feminist Latina writers, unlike the gatekeepers they depict, refuse to either acculturate or assimilate to both cultures. Instead they carefully pick and choose what "ideologies" they wish to expose as detrimental for women in both cultures.

They make their choices without making the mistakes of some feminist theorists who substitute the Enlightenment/patriarchal perspective for an essentialist feminist perspective and who substitute "the view from nowhere with the view from womanland" (Romany 1995, 391). For Latina writers' texts are never just expressing a simplistic, "essentialist standpoint of the silenced woman" (Romany 1995, 393). They are describing women of color encumbered by many layers of oppression. In addition, their texts are organized/structured for the most part by what they are attempting to expose in terms of inequitable gendered, raced, and class relations of power in both cultures as mediated and enforced through gatekeepers.

All the authors analyzed in this text also frequently depict issues involving "acculturation" and "assimilation" as themes:

> Although no definitional agreement exists, assimilation usually refers to the complete loss of the original ethnic identity, as the person is absorbed into the dominant culture. Assimilation can thus be perceived, from a

minority perspective, as a pejorative term implying abandonment of traditional Hispanic values. Acculturation, however, is a multifaceted and gradual process. In the past, acculturation and assimilation were often interrelated, but the emphasis today is beginning to shift toward bicultural or multicultural acculturation; that is, an individual being able to participate actively in several cultures without having to negate one's ethnic identity. (Domino 1995, 57)

Thus Latina writers frequently propose "hybridity" and "syncretism" as solutions to the problem of assimilation. In George Domino's opinion, these are the best available models for ridding their characters of "unproductive polarizations" that inhere in essentialist "narratives of difference" (1995, 57). In this text I analyze how Cofer's distinctions between her mother and father as binaries enable readers to comprehend the complexity of her biculturalism, hybridity, and syncresis. Not only Cofer. All the Latina writers explored in this text object to assimilation or acculturation models by depicting their heroines' torturous quests to find personal meaning and fulfillment in their lives through their insistence on retaining their cultural identity. We also see the authors offering a variety of differing solutions to the issues of assimilation and acculturation. Ramis details the successful struggles for a Puerto Rican identity in both the unyielding nationalistic revolutionary Uncle Sergio and the bicultural, hybridized, and syncretized narrator, Lidia. The Dominican Julia Alvarez depicts her character Laura Garcia de la Torre as consciously assimilating and acculturating into American ways minimally—only to the extent she thinks will benefit her personal agenda of self-fulfillment. The Cubana, Cristina Garcia, through her American-born feminist character Pilar, describes her ultimately successful search for psychic integration of her Americanness and Cubanness through "dreaming in Cuban," through psychic communion with her communist Cuban grandmother.

It appears to me that the psychic condition that Anouar Majid defines as "hybridity and syncretism" stems from Latinas' sense of "enforced psychic tourism" in terms of inequitable gendered power relations in our world. The conditions of "hybridity and syncretism" reflect choice, a significant difference from "enforced psychic tourism," although not always admired. To propagate them unthinkingly leaves those who do so with the risk of "becoming complicitous with the systemic violence inflicted on billions of people worldwide" (1996, 17) because hybridity and syncretism reflect the unself-reflexive perspective "of most diasporic Third World intellectuals" (1996, 17). Suffering "stoically" (1996, 17), they ceaselessly attempt to find a psychic home between a birthplace "that is no longer theirs" and a new home in the west.

Majid concludes with a description of such intellectuals that resonates profoundly, unforgettably for me: the first description I ever encountered in all my reading that matches my own past and current condition of "homelessness-as-home, home-as-homelessness" (Majid 1996, 17). Ironically, he meant this description to apply to Middle Eastern, Third World scholars and Americans of color, not to a descendant of the Jewish diaspora from Cossack pogroms in Eastern Europe.

Critical of any members of his group who conform to and internalize western ways, Majid condemns their hybridization and syncretization. He sees such attempts as playing into the ethnocentrism of the "Western academic apparatus" which can then unjustifiably congratulate itself on its dubious "cultural achievement" at the expense of "the unmitigated pain of both Westernized intellectuals and indigenous peoples" (1996, 17). Once members of these groups become academics in the "Western academic apparatus," they are then bound by "the imperatives of a narrow professionalism that insists on productivity" and not on "genuine emancipation" (1996, 18). I feel more sanguine however. Ethnic and women of color feminists such as myself, and even mainstream feminists, have done hard labor for years in this "Western academic apparatus." We feminists never ceased to struggle for change from within. In the recent and ongoing canon warfare, we dodged through the traditional minefields, expanding and transforming the narrow, provincial Eurocentric university curriculum. The mortality rate was enormous, for many of us were crucified and fired before achieving tenure for attempting to integrate our feminist perspectives into the curriculum. In the process we underwent withering fire from some very big guns, and still do. Nevertheless, I personally have experienced some movement toward "genuine emancipation," integrating feminist theory with a more global perspective in the academy. By the end of the twentieth century, Majid, after all, had his essay published in an academic journal emanating from Johns Hopkins University Press, and I had my works published in academic journals and presses, as well.

Aurora Levins Morales, in her poem "Child of the Americas," expresses a far more positive attitude than Majid's, one in the same mood as Emma Lazurus's, but from a hybridized and syncretized child of the late twentieth century. According to Lourdes Rojas, Morales views herself both as multidimensional as a female and multiracial, as "culturally and socially, rooted in an integrated plurality . . . a cohesive and meaningful voice for the powerful heterogeneity of . . . immigrant women" (1989, 175). Morales's perspective represents the model for the most expansive and yet inclusive worldview that could be expressed by Latina writers. She describes them as "not so much people in the process of leaving one world and entering another as they are people living in two worlds at once" (1989, 175). But Morales, "a child of the Americas," lives in many more worlds than two simultaneously. She is truly global in her philosophical reach, perhaps because she herself embodies diverse, yet syncretized elements. She is a Jewish Puerto Rican American, out of the New York ghettos, and the descendant of immigrants. She is simultaneously "Caribeña," but not African or "taína," or European, although she has African, "taína" and European in her blood. All these genetic elements course through her, but she is a hybridized, syncretic combination. She is new. English is her "passion," Spanish is part of her "flesh," and "[S]panglish" is her first language. In her blood runs the "crossroads" of cultures into which she is born. And she is "whole" (1995, 79). Morales also sees multiple identity as a triumphant source of inspiration and pleasure for herself as an individual.

Still, it cannot be denied that multiple identity continues to recur as a problematic in one guise or another in the work of most Latina writers. Can the suffering from being forced to leave one culture, one's originary home in the world, to enter into another, ever be integrated? Both birth culture and Anglo world are equally alien in regard to the oppressive treatment of Latinas by gender, class, and race. Yet Latinas are forced to observe both cultures from outside their class systems by virtue of being women born into those cultures. This excess, beyond and yet contained within "hybridity and syncretism," is precisely where "psychic enforced tourism" lies. Needless to say, this experience is common to the Latina authors analyzed in this text, as well as to most ethnic and women of color writers.

Always, perhaps more than any other issue in their lives, Anglo culture reinforces in Latinas their original culture's construction of power relations through class rankings by gender and race. What de la Torre and Pesquera claim is characteristic of Chicana writers is also characteristic of Latina writers, as well. "Chicanas are not only questioning and restructuring feminist and national discourses but also infusing largely unexplored class themes with new forms of identity that have until now been absent from Chicano/a cultural productions . . . by incorporating sex/gender domination and resistance within a colonial dialectic" (1993, 3, 6). To expand this paradigm globally, ethnics and people of color are always placed in subordinate positions in terms of class compared with those in power who are always males, "for all categories are, as [Judith] Butler and others have put it, 'regulatory regimes'"(Walters 1996, 851). Simultaneously, women of all races and classes are always "constructed in power relations" (Walters 1996, 851), that is, in subordinate positions to white men in all cultures where white men rule, when a "white, bourgeois, and masculine fetishistic imaginary reigns" (Walters 1996, 854). However, Walters fails to observe that even in cultures where men of color rule, women of color are situated in subordinate positions in real life, as well as depicted as subordinate to male characters in their literature. I do agree with Walters and Romany however, that everywhere on the planet in every culture, "lines of power . . . mark themselves on the lives of gendered, raced, ethnic subjects." This is done, not only conceptually, ideologically, discursively, but "at the very concrete level of power differentials and unequal distributions of privileges" (Walters 1996, 863; Romany 1995, 395).

All the Latina writers analyzed in this text respond to their firsthand experiences of inequitable gendered power relations with attempts to analyze the patriarchy's diverse manifestations and to oppose its domination wherever those manifestations present themselves. That is, everywhere, from the bed to the boardroom, as the saying goes, except that no Latina authors depict their Latina characters in boardrooms. Rather, they depict their Latina characters as bored in rooms that confine them, in factories, fast-food restaurants, or domestic spaces, for the most part. Latina writers depict the enforcement of inequitable gendered power relations in females from the moment when Latina children begin their training under their gatekeepers at home, again in school, and again when they migrate psychically to the workplace and physically to the United States. They are faced with and forced to conform to racist, sexist, and class oppression all their lives, within and beyond their birth cultures.

To find a "space" to vent their rage, Latina writers often choose to do it through violent characters, images, and scenes in their writing. This is a characteristic fairly common among writers from oppressed groups, especially feminist writers, and not only unique to Latina writers. Aurora Levins Morales's work fits this model. She became a feminist in the course of consciousness-raising sessions "in those rooms of women leaning intently toward each other" (1995, 807). She began to feel "indignation," an emotion that "became an anchor" for her in that it sourced her writing as an adult. "Not the poems and fables of my childhood, but thick, black journals full of confusion, like a howling wind, where I raged and mourned and thought and planned, reaching for the clear place, the eye at the heart of the storm" (1995, 807).

Ana Lydia Vega also testifies to the same source for her writing. She believes that the experiences she has had since infancy "with repression, this constant negotiation with a male-dominated world leaves an imprint on one's self." Vega claims that it is not necessary to read feminist theories in order to know them, to be a feminist in practice, to arrive at some positions that frame what one chooses to write about. Although she did study feminist theory while attending university, her feminism strikes her as "more a response to decisions I have made in my life [that] grew out of decisions and positions that are lived experiences" ("Interview," Hernández and López Springfield, 1994, 816-817). In this sense, many of the works of Latina authors can be defined as in the genre of "revenge narratives . . . that . . . unmask patriarchy—lays it bare—in a way that avenges at least some of the wrongs done to women in its name" (Vélez 1988, 2). In addition, as Frederick Jameson has noted about "Third World literature," it "tends to be satirical and allegorical" (1986, 69). This is also a characteristic of the Latina authors I analyze in this text. They frequently vent their rage through irony, satire, and allegory.

Finally, Latina authors convey a perspective about inequitable gendered power relations different from any of their characters, male and female. Unlike their characters, the authors' perspective toward their culture(s) is current at the historical moment in which they are writing their texts, as opposed to that of their troubled characters. The authors' perspective is feminist, informed by a conscious, feminist critique of inequitable power relations in terms of class as grounded in and emanating from cultural gendered and raced constructions. Unlike their characters, the Latina writers are entirely conscious of and confront the awful reality: "the self-affirmation of one class [men] . . . as a means of social control and political subjugation" (Foucault 1990, 123). This is also the perspective from which I have written this work . . . defines this perspective as one that "looks at women as a class oppressed by material conditions and social relations . . . [T]herefore, rather than considering gender polarization as the victimization of only women, material feminism considers it a social construct oppressive to both women and men" (Boesing citing Dolan 1996, 1019).

As if they were writing "ethnographies . . . of their own lives" (Gwin 1996, 874), Latina writers critique their past: their original Latino, and then, sooner or later, Anglo cultures, which have constrained women, ethnic women, and women of color from full expression of their humanity. Both cultures practice what even recent American legal reports define as "systemic discrimination, disparities in treatment [that] do appear to correlate with membership in minority groups and 'even' with gender" (Resnik 1996, 959). In their current critiques, Latina authors, unlike their characters, are now aware of the vast networks and systems of belief that inevitably "engender relations of power within the social order" (as cited in Gwin 1996, 875). Even if all that Latina writers are aiming at in their works is to oppose gendered and raced power relations, at the very least, "contesting the concepts is a benefit. It is the first step" (Bunch in Hartmann et al. 1996, 941).

Another recurring theme with Latina authors, especially Ferré in *The Youngest Doll* and Garcia in *Dreaming in Cuban*, involves economics. In fact, this theme is prevalent with most feminist writers because the experience of poverty is prevalent in women's lives in a variety of ways. Rivera-Ramos expresses a position common to Latina writers:

> It is necessary to bring forth a deep change in attitudes both in the male and female populations. . . . This necessary change in traditional attitudes and ideological framework that conceptualize the white Anglo-Saxon Protestant male as the best model to copy and impose and that conceptualize women and particularly Hispanic and Puerto Rican women as the inferior part of humankind will have to be brought about in order to pave the way toward the optimization of economic growth and development. (1995, 195)

Another element so common in the Latina authors that I have made it the major focus of my analysis in this text is the implication of senior women in Puerto Rican and other cultures as cultural collaborationists, as gatekeepers. Latina writers depict these gatekeepers as the group that perpetuates the patriarchal rules and regulations, acting as their custodians, like vigilant watchdogs. I have chosen *Silent Dancing* as my anchor work because it so brilliantly illustrates the major thesis of my book's title, *Saddling La Gringa*, the role of gatekeepers in perpetuating inequitable gendered power relations. The phrase is used by Cofer's mother as a cautionary tale in *Silent Dancing* to sarcastically describe what happened to a young Puertorriqueña relative, influenced by the mainland culture. She tried to overstep the bounds of her culture's limits for young females, to act like a "gringa" or white woman. Gatekeepers do their cultural work primarily by narrating to their young charges "real-life stories . . . always embellishing them with a little or a lot of dramatical detail." These cuentos [stories] are shamelessly used as propaganda, as "morality and cautionary tales" (Cofer 1990, 4–5) in order to inscribe what gatekeepers deem culturally appropriate female gender roles into their young charges. I have also chosen to feature Cofer's *Silent Dancing* because it incorporates within its pages all the other major elements I previously listed.

Understandably, Latina authors are riddled with ambivalence about their foremother gatekeepers because they are simultaneously nurturers to their culture's female children while serving them as cultural censors and guides into the prisonhouse of adult womanhood in a dystopic patriarchy. Older women—mothers and grandmothers, aunts, teachers, nuns, family members, friends, and neighbors—form loyal cadres of volunteers who train children to be obedient to and serve all the interconnected institutions of traditional patriarchy. They conscientiously pour the young into cultural molds, teaching them to be terrified of breaking the rules on pain of religious, legal, political, economic, educational, social, cultural, community, and family ostracism, even unto death.

I also stress *Silent Dancing* because Cofer's "persistent questioning of . . . the concept of bourgeois motherhood" provides the exemplar for illustrating the role of gatekeepers in other Latina writers, the concept "that defines the mother both in and by her domestic role: passive, submissive, servile, and silent in front of men. In such a definition, the mother is seen as an intermediary for men but never as an active agent of her own life or that of her descendants" (Ortega 1989, 127–128). Eliana Ortega makes these comments only about Puerto Rican women's "poetic discourse." Nevertheless, she could well be summarizing the responses of other Latina writers to inequitable gendered power relations in terms of women's roles. They are committed to "demythify the patriarchal discourse of dominant culture" (1989, 129) through demythifying the role of mother/foremother as gatekeeper. That Ortega notes this response as "subversive" adds a feminist dimension and complexity to the too-often essentialized (and misguided) paeans to foremothers and mothers that critics have tended to make. They assume worshipful poses at the very sight of mother/foremother figures in the works of Latina writers, even though to some large extent they are depicted negatively or with great ambivalence as gatekeepers of Latino and Anglo culture's inequitable gendered power relations.

SELECTED BIBLIOGRAPHY

Bilbija, Kisenija. 1994. "Rosario Ferre's 'The Youngest Doll': On Women, Dolls, Golems and Cyborgs." *Callaloo* 17.3: 878–888.

Boesing, Martha. 1996. "Rushing Headlong into the Fire at the Foot of the Mountain." *Signs: Journal of Women in Culture and Society. Special Issue Edition: Feminist Theory and Practice* 21(4): 1011–1023.

Bruce-Novoa, Juan. 1989. "Deconstructing the Dominant Patriarchal Text: Cecile Pineda's Narratives" In *Breaking Boundaries: Latina Writing and Critical Readings,* ed. Asunción Horno-Delgado, Eliana Ortega, Nina M. Scott, and Nancy Saporta Sternbach, 72–81. Amherst: University of Massachusetts Press.

Cofer, Judith Ortiz. 1990. *Silent Dancing: A Partial Remembrance of a Puerto Rican Childhood.* Houston: Arte Publico Press.

de la Torre, Adela, and Beatriz M. Pesquera, ed. 1993. *Building With Our Hands: New Directions in Chicana Studies.* Berkeley: University of California Press.

Dewey, Janice. 1989. "Doña Josefa: Bloodpulse of Transition and Change." In *Breaking Boundaries: Latina Writing and Critical Readings,* ed. Asunción Horno-Delgado, Eliana Ortega, Nina M. Scott, and Nancy Saporta Sternbach, 39–47. Amherst: University of Massachusetts Press.

Domino, George. 1995. "Acculturation of Hispanics." In *Hispanics in the Workplace,* ed. Stephen B. Knouse, Paul Rosenfeld, and Amy L. Culbertson, 56–74. Newbury Park, CA: Sage Publications.

Ferré, Rosario, 1994. "The Bitches' Colloquy." *Callaloo* 17(3): 889–899.

Foucault, Michel. 1990. *The History of Sexuality, Volume 1: An Introduction,* trans. Robert Hurley. New York: Vintage.

Gwin, Minrose. 1996. "Space Travel: The Connective Politics of Feminist Reading." *Signs: Journal of Women in Culture and Society* 21(4): 870–905.

Haaken, Janice. 1996. "The Recovery of Memory, Fantasy, and Desire: Feminist Approaches to Sexual Abuse and Psychic Drama." *Signs: Journal of Women in Culture and Society* 21(4): 1069–1091.

Hartmann, Heidi, Ellen Bravo, et al. 1996. "Bringing Together Feminist Theory and Practice: A Collective Interview," *Signs: Journal of Women in Culture and Society* 21(4): 917–951.

Horno-Delgado, Asunción, Eliana Ortega, Nina M. Scott, and Nancy Saporta Sternbach, eds. 1989a. *Breaking Boundaries: Latina Writing and Critical Readings.* Amherst: University of Massachusetts Press.

Horno-Delgado, Asunción. 1989b. "Señores, don't leibol me, please!!: ya soy Luz María Umpierre." *Breaking Boundaries: Latina Writing and Critical Readings,* ed. Asunción Horno-Delgado, Eliana Ortega, Nina M. Scott, and Nancy Saporta Sternbach, trans. Janet N. Gold, 136–145. Amherst: University of Massachusetts Press.

Jameson, Frederic. 1986. "Third World Literature in the Era of Multinational Capitalism." *Social Text* 15: 65–88.

Kutzinski, Vera M. 1993. *Sugar's Secrets: Race and the Erotics of Cuban Nationalism.* Charlottesville: University Press of Virginia.

López Springfield, Consuelo. 1994. " 'I am the life, the Strength, the Woman': Feminism in Julia de Burgos' Autobiographical Poetry." *Callaloo* 17(3): 701–714.

Majid, Anouar. 1996. "Can the Postcolonial Critic Speak? Orientalism and the Rushdie Affair." *Cultural Critique* 32: 5–42.

Morales, Aurora Levins. 1995. "Child of the Americas" from *Getting Home Alive* by Aurora Levins Morales and Rosario Morales. In *Boriquas: Influential Puerto Rican Writings–An Anthology,* ed. Robert Santiago, 79. New York: One World/Ballantine Books.

Ortega, Eliana. 1989. "Poetic Discourse of the Puerto Rican Woman in the U.S.: New Voices of Anacoanian Liberation." In *Breaking Boundaries: Latina Writing and Critical Readings,* ed. Asunción Horno-Delgado, Eliana Ortega, Nina M. Scott, and Nancy Saporta Sternbach, 122–135. Amherst: University of Massachusetts Press.

Resnik, Judith. 1996. "Asking about Gender in Courts." *Signs: Journal of Women in Culture and Society* 21(4): 952–990.

Rivera-Ramos, Alba N. 1995. "The Psychological Experience of Puerto Rican Women at Work." In *Hispanics in the Workplace,* ed. Stephen B. Knouse, Paul Rosenfeld, and Amy L. Culbertson, 194–207. Newbury Park, CA and London: Sage Publications.

Rojas, Lourdes. 1989. "Latinas at the Crossroads: An Affirmation of Life in Rosario Morales and Aurora Levins Morales' *Getting Home Alive.*" In *Breaking Boundaries: Latina Writing and Critical Readings,* ed. Asunción Horno-Delgado, Eliana Ortega, Nina M. Scott, and Nancy Saporta Sternbach, 166–180. Amherst: University of Massachusetts Press.

Romany, Celina. 1995. "Ain't I a Feminist?" In *Latinas in the United States: History, Law and Perspective,* Volume 2, *Latina Issues: Fragments of Historia (Ella) (Herstor).* ed.

Antoinette Sedillo López. 389–399. New York and London: Garland Press. (Orig. ptd. in *Yale Journal of Law and Feminism.*)

Scorczewski, Dawn. 1996. "What Prison Is This? Literary Critics Cover Incest in Anne Sexton's 'Briar Rose.' " *Signs: Journal of Women in Culture and Society* 21(2): 309–342.

Sternbach, Nancy Saporta. 1989. In *Breaking Boundaries: Latina Writing and Critical Readings,* ed. Asunción Horno-Delgado, Eliana Ortega, Nina M. Scott, and Nancy Saporta Sternbach, 48–61. Amherst: University of Massachusetts Press.

Vargas, Yamila Azize. 1989. "A Commentary on the Works of Three Puerto Rican Women Poets in New York," trans. Sonia Crespo Vega. In *Breaking Boundaries: Latina Writing and Critical Readings,* ed. Asunción Horno-Delgado, Eliana Ortega, Nina M. Scott, and Nancy Saporta Sternbach, 146–165. Amherst: University of Massachusetts Press.

Vélez, Diana L. 1988. Reclaiming Medusa: Short Stories by Contemporary Puerto Rican Women Writers. San Francisco: Spinsters/Aunt Lute.

Walters, Suzanna Danuta. 1996. "From Here to Queer: Radical Feminism, Postmodernism, and the Lesbian Menace (Or, Why Can't a Woman Be More Like a Fag?)." In *Feminist Theory and Practice,* ed. Barbara Christian, et al., special issue of *Signs: Journal of Women in Culture and Society* 21(4): 830–869.

CHICANA FEMINIST CRITICISM

Debra A. Castillo

Until very recently, scholars working in Chicana studies have had to pay their dues to the establishment by first pursuing a research specialization in a non-U.S. hispanophone literature (for example, Tey Diana Rebolledo and Norma Alarcón both did Ph.D. dissertations on Mexican poet and feminist Rosario Castellanos, and Elizabeth Ordóñez studied women from Spain) or in a canonical U.S. English area of study. Others, like Gloria Anzaldúa, have intentionally eschewed the traditional academic credentialing process. Thus, unlike the current, younger generation of thinkers, the women who entered the profession in the 1970s and 1980s, founding the Chicano Studies programs and establishing journals and presses, had to do much of their most important early work outside (and often with resistance from) the institutional channels, and without either recognition or reward. The consequences of this academic myopia on the part of the dominant culture are manifold. Until astonishingly recently, anglophone Chicana literature has been institutionally homeless, perceived as marginal or second rate, and thus not respected within English Department circles. Hispanophone Chicana literature has been seen as culturally contaminated, written in "bad Spanish," and certainly not appropriate for (Latin) American literature courses. Critics who write on such works have therefore been marginalized as well, and have been continually on the defensive, having to define and redefine their field of interest, justify it to the academic community as a valid and exciting area of study, and then, finally, begin to lay the groundwork of serious analysis. These are severe handicaps for any field, and help explain the strong anti-institutional thread and oppositional rhetoric in much of the most well-known Chicana feminist thought.

The Mexican literary establishment has, unfortunately, been similarly reluctant to take into account the contributions and potentiality of a dialogue between Mexican and Chicana scholars. In fact, one of the strongest criticisms made regarding the III Border Seminar, "Mujer y literatura Mexicana

From *Latino and Latina Writers* Edition 1 (Scribner Writers Series), 1st edition by Alan West–Duran (Editor), Alan West (Editor). 2002. Reprinted with permission of Gale, a division of Thompson Learning: www.thompsonrights.com. Fax 800 730-2215.

y Chicana: Culturas en contacto," which took place in Tijuana, Mexico, in May 1989, addressed the lack of comparative analysis among Mexican and Chicana women. Alarcón, discussing one of the uncomfortable confrontations at that event in her article "Cognitive Desires: An Allegory of/for Chicana Critics," warns of an increasingly vast distance between Mexicans and Chicanas, precisely at the point in which contact and exchange could be most fruitful. "We became spectators to a textual performative that claimed to incorporate us. . . . Thus Chicanas were placed in a negative position whereby if they had wanted to speak it would have been to note their exclusion from an event that supposedly included them in the conference's goals" (*Chicana (W)rites: On Word and Film*, pp. 191–192). Obvious but often unspoken class and race differences lie at the bottom of much of this distance, Alarcón finds, as the Mexican women are whiter and higher class than their browner, working-class origin Chicana counterparts.

Curiously enough, in recent years one could almost say that the situation has been reversed, and that Chicana feminist thinkers and writers are now the pre-eminent figures in the field, far surpassing in influence their male counterparts. And the field itself has more than confirmed its intellectual force, with strong institutional advocates in the United States, Europe, Australia, and Asia. Even in Mexico, where resistance to *pochos* (acculturated Chicanas) has often been high, Chicana writers' works are now widely available in Spanish translation, and prominent social critics like Elena Poniatowska and Carlos Monsiváis have spoken and written extensively about the real and potential contribution of vital Chicana thinking to the Mexican imaginary. This high degree of recognition is particularly true of the strong generation of women writers forged in the crucible of a double resistance: on the one hand, an early lack of academic respect for their work; on the other, the disapproval of the male leadership of the oppositional Chicano movement. These women are the most cited of the feminist critics and their efforts have provided the groundwork for the field of Chicana studies as a whole; thus, they are also the focus of this article. Norma Alarcón, Gloria Anzaldúa, Ana Castillo, Cherríe Moraga, and Chela Sandoval must be taken into account in any evaluation of the status of Chicana feminist thought. More forcefully, one should argue that these women need to be included in any evaluation of Chicano thought in general, and into any evaluation of contemporary U.S. thought.

As Norma Alarcón notes in one of her essays, "Since the emergence of Chicana critics can be traced no further back than about 1965, applying the name retroactively is a reconstruction of a chosen gene(an)alogy, much like calling Sor Juan Inés de la Cruz a Modern Woman" ("Cognitive Desires," pp. 186–187). In tracing this genealogy, today's scholars necessarily recognize their debts to activists that include Rosaura Sánchez, Linda Apodaca, Martha Cotera, Mary Helen Alvarado, Sonia López, Mary Lou Espinosa, Ana Nieto Gómez, Francisca Flores, and Marta Vidal. Yet, because much of these women's work is directly activist rather than presented in traditional scholarly formats, and because it tended to be published in journals and small magazines of limited circulation like the *Revista Chicana-Riqueña* (now *Americas Review*), *El Grito*, *ChismeArte*, or *La Cosecha*, their writings have only recently begun to receive the attention due them. Fortunately, through the publication of recent anthologies like Alma Garcia's *Chicana Feminist Thought*, crucial works by these foremothers are now more widely available.

Fundamentally then, Chicana feminist theory and criticism as a body of analysis is of relatively recent vintage, and, like Alarcón, most scholars point to the activist days of the 1960s as the starting point for this academic field of study. Armando Rendón's *The Chicano Manifesto*, often seen as a defining statement for the Chicano movement in general, dates from 1971, and a contemporary perusal of this historic document reminds today's readers of the often bitter conflicts between male leaders who frequently rejected the legitimacy of Chicana struggles and women activists who saw the profound contradictions in a political struggle that left women behind. Rendón evokes heroic figures like the Mexican Revolutionary generals Emiliano Zapata and Pancho Villa as models for contemporary political praxis and as models of a virile leadership. At the heart of Rendón's document is a strong statement that identifies machismo as a positive ideology and as the symbolic organizing principle for Chicano family life. This combination of revolutionary rhetoric and traditional family values leaves very little space for independent and powerful women who reject the traditional supportive roles of wife and mother as their only proper sphere of involvement. Tellingly, the movement leaders evince a considerable suspicion of and nervousness about the potential participation of their Chicana counterparts.

Thus, in Rendón's famous document, the Chicano activist represents a (male) political force for positive change; as Angie Chabram-Dernersesian writes in her essay "I Throw Punches for My Race, but I Don't Want to Be a Man: Writing Us—Chica-nos (Girl, Us)/Chicanas—into the Movement Script," "he grounds his symbolic treatment of machismo in a specific male body, equating macho with Chicano, a term generalized to embrace the nationalist objective" (*Cultural Studies: A Critical Reader*, p. 83). The Chicana, on the other hand, has "thus been removed from full-scale participation in the Chicano movement as fully embodied, fully empowered U.S. Mexican female subjects. They are not only engendered under machismo but their gender is disfigured at the symbolic level under malinchismo" ("I Throw Punches for My Race," p. 83). On a more mundane level, as Adelaida del Castillo recalls in "Mexican Women in Organization," even when women provided the major organizing force for local movements, they were forced to defer to a male figurehead as the visible representative of their group—this was a lose-lose situation: "Commonly women in leadership were labeled unfeminine or deviant. . . . When a woman leader had a compañero, he was frequently taunted or reprimanded by the other men for failure to keep her under his control" (*Mexican Women in the United States*, pp. 8–9).

It is not surprising, thus, that Chicana activists rejected this exclusionary discourse, along with the male domination of the political movement, and their relegation to traditional roles in the *familia*. Cherríe Moraga says it succinctly in *The Last Generation*:

> For a generation, nationalist leaders used a kind of "selective memory,"
> drawing exclusively from those aspects of Mexican and Native cultures

that served the interests of male heterosexuals. At times, they took the worse of Mexican machismo and Aztec warrior bravado, combined it with some of the most oppressive male-conceived idealizations of "traditional" Mexican womanhood and called that cultural integrity. (pp. 156–157)

Similarly, Aida Hurtado critiques the 1960s movement for its lack of sensitivity to gender issues—this is in fact one of the three "blasphemies" explored in her 1996 book *The Color of Privilege: Three Blasphemies on Race and Feminism*. In her "Manifestación tardía" (Belated manifesto), Margarita Cota-Cárdenas argues passionately for rethinking militancy as derived from the Chicano movement frame, and for writing women more definitively into the movement script as full partners, as *hermanas* (sisters), as Chicanas, as *mujeres* (women) in the full sense of the term. She notes that it is not sufficient to replace the "o" at the end of "Chicano" with the letter "a"; instead, activist Chicanas need to imagine new social relations, new subjectivities, and new strategies of interaction. Cota-Cárdenas's reflection, published in 1980, anticipates the work of her fellow Chicana activists and scholars during the blossoming of Chicana scholarship in the 1980s and 1990s.

From a more contemporary perspective, we know that these Chicanas, formed in the crucible of movement politics, and often reviled as *malinchistas* (a slur referring to the mistress and translator of Spanish conquerer Hernán Cortés meaning race traitor) and *vendidas* (sell outs), by their male counterparts, have been crucial in setting the groundwork for a specifically Chicana feminism, for re-evaluating the symbolic structures of Malinche and Guadalupe, and for claiming for themselves a source of pride in coming from a long line of *vendidas*. La Chicana, then, in the more developed sense anticipated by Cota-Cárdenas, becomes an important concept for helping think through these new subjectivities. At the same time, says Tey Diana Rebolledo in her 1995 book *Women Singing in the Snow*, the problem for Chicanas is specifically how to imagine these new subjectivities given a long history of silence:

The problems and multiple answers to "Who am I? How do I see myself, How am I seen by others?" are thus constantly being refigured and repositioned, so the issue of "identity" in feminist work is one that will not go away. On a wider scale . . . it is not only a question of the individual processes of "subject positioning" but also one of ideological processes that are fully implicated in social formations of the individual and the group. (p. 97)

Chicana feminists have traditionally focused on two large areas of inquiry where the political and the personal intersect: the *familia* (especially studies of expected gender roles), and the institution (social, political, religious, linguistic, academic). The Chicana's family in particular has been the focus of social, scientific, and literary studies, essays, autoethnographies, novels, stories, poems, plays, critical analysis, and sui generis mixed forms. In a nutshell, the basic concept of the typical *familia* would be as follows: The *familia* structures itself around a self-sacrificing mother, whose power resides in her absolute control over her children as well as in the moral authority that derives from her unending suffering. The good father is neither faithful to his wife nor particularly available to his children, but he does support his family economically and observes a certain amount of discretion in his outside affairs. In the best of cases, the father is a background influence in the family, while day-to-day household decisions are made by the mother. The bad father, on the other hand, is often violent, is irresponsible with his money, drinks to excess, and also allows his wife and children to know about his philandering (this adds to the wife's suffering and thus increases her moral capital). The Chicano son is privileged and petted, a spoiled being that will grow up into a man neither to be trusted nor depended upon. He will, however, revere his mother, though he is unlikely to show respect for any other woman. The protofeminist daughter, compelled throughout childhood to serve the men in her *familia*, begins to question this traditional order and asserts her right to explore alternative family dynamics and sexual partnerships with women as well as with men.

In their analyses of the various levels of institutional culture, Chicana critics have addressed questions of politics and ideology at every level from local to global. They have explored the implications of pockets of the third world in the first, rethinking, for example, girl gangs and *maquiladora* (assembly plant) industries. They have re-evaluated and re-valorized traditional spiritual and healing practices, looking to *curanderismo* (folkhealing), *brujería* (witchcraft), and Mexican native customs for their inspiration. They have argued in favor of the full richness of Chicana linguistic expression in English, Spanish, Spanglish, and Caló. They have spoken forcefully about the shoehorning of Chicana scholarly work into an academic system that was never structured to accommodate them. Above all, these critics have explored a feminocentric writing and thinking process that interrupts the long, patriarchal monologue and contests the institutional prejudices against alternative forms of argument. At the same time, many of these women are acutely conscious of the institutional stakes in their own status as token minorities. In 1985 Carmen Tafolla warned: "Don't play 'will the Real Chicana Please Stand Up?' Much as we have heard different groups compete for 'charter membership' in the Most Oppressed Club, Deep in the Barrio Bar, Pachuca of the Year Award, Mujer Sufrida ranks, and Double Minority Bingo, we must admit that membership dues must be continuously paid and advertised" (*To Split a Human: Mitos, machos, y la mujer Chicana*, p. 175).

GLORIA ANZALDÚA

According to Rebolledo, "after Gloria Anzaldúa published *Borderlands/The New Mestiza* in 1987, Chicanas breathed a sigh of relief because the tensions, the conflict, the shiftings were finally articulated. And Anzaldúa not only defined what Chicanas had been feeling for some time, but she presented it in a positive way" (*Women Singing in the Snow*, p. 103). Strikingly, her book is both hermeneutical and performative, and its ideologically charged discourse of self-enactment electrified the Chicana community. Critics have made Gloria Anzaldúa *the* representative scholar of the U.S.–Mexican border, and no respectable work on border theory can avoid engagement with her absolutely central text. *Borderlands/La Frontera* is the mega-bestseller of Chicana theorizing, and Anzaldúa's work is read, cited, and debated in a wide range of contexts, making her one of the most quoted scholars in the United States of any ethnicity. Success brings its own challenges, of course. Anzaldúa writes about being tired of being "repeatedly tokeni[zed]" (*Making Face, Making Soul: Haciendo caras*, p. xvi) as one of the same half dozen women continually called upon as a resource, and thus drained of energy that would allow her to continue her own literary and political work.

Anzaldúa's *Borderlands* in many senses is a continuation of her lifelong task of building a woman of color feminism that is theoretical, empirical, and personal at the same time. In this project, what she calls "the new mestiza"—a mestiza being a woman of mixed European and American Indian ancestry—emerges through consciousness-raising, in the evolution of an oppositional perspective. Gloria Anzaldúa is critical of United States authoritarianism, and in her writings she challenges what she sees as the hegemony of dominant-culture U.S. discourse. For this author, theory and lived experience cannot be divided, and work best when they speak coterminously, as a coherent and embodied knowledge set. Ultimately, her goal is alliance building. Hence, while she knows that her work is much discussed among scholars and critics (and agrees that for her part she finds abstract theoretical language seductive), she makes a special effort to reach out to nonacademics. Likewise, she emphasizes support for the work of women of color in general, including those who do not yet know they are writers, and she is particularly concerned by a too-common tendency among women of color to suppress each other's voices. She writes: "Nothing scares the Chicana more than a quasi Chicana; nothing disturbs a Mexican more than an acculturated Chicana; nothing agitates a Chicana more than a Latina who lumps her with the norteamericanas. It is easier to retreat to the safety of difference, behind racial, cultural, and class borders" (*Making Face, Making Soul*, p. 145). These are precisely the borders she wants to break down. Speaking of her anthology, Anzaldúa says she is "acutely conscious of the politics of address. *Haciendo caras* addresses a feminist readership of all ethnicities and both genders—yes, men too. Contrary to the norm, it does not address itself *primarily* to whites, but invites them to 'listen in' to women-of-color talking to each other and, in some instances, to and 'against' white people" (p. xviii). Later in the same text she adds, "mujeres-de-color speak and write not just against traditional white ways and texts but against a prevailing mode of being, against a white frame of reference" (p. xxii). This white frame of reference also includes pressure to write and speak in standard English rather than to use code-switching or Spanish. For this reason, Anzaldúa eschews familiar, dominant culture forms of theorizing, and peppers her language with key words and phrases in her own Tex–Mex Spanish. An engagement with the borders of language in all their senses is among Anzaldúa's most persistent images; she is, we recall, a poet as well as a theorist.

To address the inequities she sees from other grounds—from an alternative perspective—she draws heavily from indigenous myth, leading up to a celebration of the indigenous part of her mestiza heritage. In another move, she describes a symbolic equivalence between the border and her body. In a much quoted poetic passage in *Borderlands*, for instance, she describes the geopolitical line as "una herida abierta" (an open wound), a:

> 1,950 mile-long open wound
> . . . .
> running down the length of my body,
> staking fence rods in my flesh,
> . . . .
> me raja me raja. (pp. 2–3)

In Anzaldúa's work the border functions primarily as a metaphor, in that the border space as a geopolitical region converges with discourses of ethnicity, class, language, gender, and sexual preference.

Borderlands/La Frontera consists of two parts, each with seven chapters. The first part, entitled "Atravesando fronteras/Crossing Borders," is the most frequently read and discussed part of the book; it consists of a sui generis mix of historical, personal, and poetic reflections leading up to a passionate call to a Chicana self-empowerment. The second half, entitled "Un agitado viento/ Ehécatl, the Wind" rearticulates her theoretical positions in even more lyric form, privileging politically charged poetry. Drawing on one of Anzaldúa's principal metaphors, critics have sometimes described this book as serpentine. Certainly it does not offer an argument in the traditional, Western form, but rather proposes something closer to a spiritual journey, and one that frequently reflects upon Nahua/Aztec goddesses whose names and attributes contain the word for serpent, "coatl." Anzaldúa's trip begins in Aztlán, the mythic Aztec homeland, offering a capsule history of south Texas from the original peopling of the Americas to her own family's sharecropper history. Here, *Borderlands'* perspective closely approximates the everyday life of the primary cultures of the valley of Texas. In this part of her book, Anzaldúa articulates a cultural and social wall between white Americans and Mexican Americans. She describes how the Texan brand of capitalism has made its mark by dispossessing the valley's inhabitants who seem, from an Anglo perspective, strange and stubborn persons. At the same time, and as is typical in Anzaldúa, the Anglo perspective is itself distanced and mediated, seen through the eyes of the oppressed who then reinterpret it to contest oppression.

In U.S. dominant culture terms, says Anzaldúa, "Borders are set up to define places that are safe and unsafe, to distinguish *us* from *them*" (*Borderlands/La Frontera*, p. 3). Clearly, in this projection, U.S. dominant culture is the normative "us"; the unsettling "them" consists of "the prohibited and the forbidden. . . . the squint-eyed, the perverse, the queer, the troublesome, the mongrel, the mulato, the half-breed, the half-dead; in short, those who cross over, pass over, or go through the confines of the 'normal'" (p. 3). It is a land distinguished by its tension, its ambivalence, its danger, and the overwhelming, constant presence of violence and death.

In subsequent chapters she explores her own oppression as a Chicana and a lesbian, and then in chapters 3–7 articulates the growth of her political and feminist consciousness, rejecting the patriarchal Aztlán for what she calls the Coatlicue state, responding to a feminist consciousness that demands new myths and new symbols. On her way to this conclusion, she rethinks such crucial culture figures as the Virgin of Guadalupe with respect to the Aztec goddess Coatlopeuh, "she who has dominion over serpents" (p. 29), and argues passionately that all Chicanos, and more urgently, all Chicanas, need to overcome the linguistic oppression that has limited the possibilities for expression to devalorized and stumbling tongues. The culminating chapter of this section of the book, the most closely read and most influential, is the final chapter of this first part: "La concienca de la mestiza/Towards a New Consciousness."

Anzaldúa's recuperation of this space begins with the myth of Aztlán, the mythical homeland of the Aztecs, a nomadic tribe that left the southwest in the twelfth century and eventually wandered south to the area of central Mexico, where they established the empire that was conquered by Hernán Cortés in the early sixteenth century. Spanish, *mestizo* (mixed blood), and indigenous conquerors then traveled back northwards in a journey of conquest to the border area: "this constituted a return to the place of origin, Aztlán, thus making Chicanos originally and secondarily indigenous to the southwest" (p. 5). Anglo *Tejanos* (Texans) brought a second conquest force to the area, and with the victory over Mexican forces in 1848 established the current borderline with the Treaty of Guadalupe–Hidalgo. While the rights of Mexican citizens were guaranteed by that treaty, the actuality of subsequent events was a shameful history of swindles and outright theft, leaving the Mexican Chicana inhabitants of the region dispossessed and feeling alien in their own land. Meanwhile, on the other side of this artificially constructed political boundary, poverty-stricken Mexicans dreamed of a better life for themselves and their families on the U.S. side of the border, and faced the dangers of illegal crossing and the humiliation of their treatment by the INS and the employers on the other side. This, says Anzaldúa, is "what Reagan calls a frontline, a war zone. The convergence has created a shock culture, a third country, a closed country" (p. 11). The entire weight of her intellectual, personal, and spiritual journey in this book is to provide a counternarrative to this story of betrayal and loss, to this culture of violence and spiritual devastation. "Don't give me your tenets and your laws," she writes. "So don't give me your lukewarm gods. What I want is an accounting with all three cultures—white, Mexican, Indian. I want the freedom to carve and chisel my own face, to staunch the bleeding with ashes, to fashion my own gods out of my entrails" (p. 22).

Because she lives in more than one culture, the new mestiza has to process conflicting messages, and she develops what Anzaldúa describes as "a tolerance for contradictions, a tolerance for ambiguity" (p. 79). The clash of cultures strengthens her tolerance and provides her with the tools to achieve a pluralistic consciousness greater than the sum of its parts. Ultimately, Anzaldúa's is a utopic project:

> The work of the mestiza consciousness is to break down the subject-object duality that keeps her a prisoner and to show in the flesh and through the images of her work how duality is transcended. . . . A massive uprooting of dualistic thinking in the individual and collective consciousness is the beginning of a long struggle, but one that could, in our best hopes, bring us to the end of rape, of violence, of war. (p. 80)

In keeping with the goddess imagery and the undertow of feminist spirituality that runs through the whole book, Anzaldúa adds: "La mestiza has gone from being the sacrificial goat to becoming the officiating priestess at the crossroads" (p. 80). Instead of rebellion and revolution in the old, death-seeking sense, in this project an evolution, "an inevitable unfolding" defines "the quickening serpent movement" (p. 81).

The new mestiza must not only officiate over these changes in herself, but, as is the function of priestesses in any spiritual practice, assist others in coming to the same crossroads. As a feminist, her task is to reinterpret patriarchal history and create a new story that privileges feminocentric, health-giving imagery. Thus, Coatlicue, the indigenous mother goddess, replaces the Spanish hybrid Virgin of Guadalupe, and the patriarchal nation-state of Aztlán gives way to the feminist Coatlicue state. This feminist project of shaping new myths with political and social resonance is most fully articulated in the central chapters of the first part of the book. In this section she first discusses the importance of the Coatlicue state as a key image in her nonlineal, serpentine form of thinking, then develops her argument about the legitimacy and expressiveness of Chicano Spanish, and argues forcefully for the role of the writer/artist in advancing this project. For the white person there is also an important task in this process: "Admit that Mexico is your double, that she exists in the shadow of this country, that we are irrevocably tied to her. Gringo, accept the doppleganger in your psyche. By taking back your collective shadow the intracultural split will heal" (p. 86).

Anzaldúa speaks from the interstices of U.S. dominant culture and she has self-authorized her hybrid discourse in the social construction of difference. Nevertheless, upon becoming the authorized and canonized voice of that difference, she is ineluctably allied to the practices of political and economic power on an international level, even given the fact that—ironically—her writing and her performative actions resist such practices. Her fertile concept of the mestiza consciousness has been exceptionally influential, and as a consequence she is frequently quoted as the premier thinker/theorist on border issues, sometimes in ways quite distant from her original project.

A typical example is Walter Mignolo's influential article, "Posoccidentalismo: el argumento desde América Latina" (Postoccidentalism: The Argument from Latin America), the Spanish version of what would become one of the key points in his later book, *Local Histories/Global Designs: Coloniality, Subaltern Knowledges, and Border Thinking* (2000). In this project, the metaphor of the border serves a crucial role. Mignolo recurs to the old Sarmientian opposition of civilization and barbarism and, tying it to an excursus on Anzaldúa, in "Posoccidentalismo" he calls for the revindication of

> la fuerza de la frontera que crea la posibilidad de la barbarie en negarse a sí misma como barbarie-en-la-otredad; de revelar la barbarie-en-la-mismidad que la categoría de civilización ocultó; y de generar un nuevo espacio de reflexión que mantiene y trasciende el concepto moderno de razón. (*Cuadernos americanos*, p. 157)

> the force of the border which creates the possibility for barbarism to deny itself as barbarism-in-otherness; to reveal the barbarism-in-the-self that the category of civilization occulted; and to generate a new space of reflection that maintains and transcends the modern concept of reason.

This is a considerable distance from Anzaldúa's Shadow Beast and Coatlicue state, especially in its complete lack of attention to Anzaldúa's strong feminist message, yet throughout his argument, as well as in the later book, Anzaldúa is credited as the guiding consciousness in Mignolo's formulation of the concept of a (genderless) border epistemology.

If the feminized border is insufficiently actualized as a conceptual tool in works like those of Mignolo, Anzaldúa poses another kind of problem for the work of other well-known border thinkers, where the concept of the borderlands can be too easily recuperated into a certain type of cultural nationalist discourse. David Johnson and Scott Michaelsen ask: "Of what use, finally, are concepts like 'culture' and 'identity' if their invocation, even in so-called multicultural contexts, is also exclusive, colonial, intolerant?" (*Border Theory: The Limits of Cultural Politics*, p. 29). On the U.S. side, the contributors to Johnson and Michaelsen's border theory volume quite rightly question, as the editors note, "the *value* of the border, both as cultural indicator and as a conceptual tool," finding "the identity politics of border studies' most prominent instantiations naive and wanting in quite similar ways" (pp. 29, 31). Benjamin Alire Saenz trenchantly argues this point from another perspective in his critique of Anzaldúa's canonical text, *Borderlands/La Frontera,* which he sees as a dangerously escapist romanticization of indigenous cultures, offering little of practical value to today's urban Chicanas.

Another critique is that *Borderlands/La Frontera*, despite its multiple crossings of cultural and gender borders—from ethnicity to feminisms, from the academic realm to the world of blue-collar labor—tends to essentialize relations between Mexico and the U.S.–Mexican border. Scholars like María-Socorro Tabuenca Córdoba have noted that Anzaldúa's transnational commentary strangely omits any concrete reference to the Mexican side of the border despite continually evoking its metaphorical presence. Her third country between the two nations, the binational borderlands, is still a metaphorical country defined and narrated from a first world perspective. Even her primary indigenous imagery is drawn not from the northern Mexico/southwestern U.S. indigenous nations, but, tellingly, from the central Mexican imaginary, invoking the Aztec imperial power (which, in pre-Columbian times, as in

the present, has had tremendously strained relations with the north). By defining her referents solely in terms of an outcast status in the United States,
Anzaldúa's famous analysis does not take into account the many other other-
nesses related to a border existence; her "us" is limited to U.S. minorities; her
"them" is U.S. dominant culture. Tabuenca Córdoba reminds her readers that
Mexican border dwellers are also "us" and "them" with respect to their Chicana counterparts; they can in some sense be considered the "other" of both
dominant and U.S. resistance discourses. It is in no wise the same, however, to
belong to an official minority within the United States as it is in Mexico.

CHERRÍE MORAGA

Californian Cherríe Moraga is a frequent collaborator with Gloría Anzaldúa,
and their work together is often spoken of as reflecting the most important
axis of Chicana feminist, and especially Chicana lesbian thought. She is well
known as the coeditor of crucial volumes of women-of-color writing, and is a
prize-winning playwright and poet as well as a theorist and essayist. Her theoretical work—from the 1983 *Loving in the War Years: Lo que nunca pasó por
sus labios* (What never passed through her lips), which still remains fresh and
pertinent, to her 1993 *The Last Generation*—comprises a continuum of un-
compromisingly political and social theorizing and poeticizing. Displaying a
similar genre-bending style as Anzaldúa, she combines poetry with political
autobiography and more abstract meditations. Also like Anzaldúa she focuses
much of her attention on reevaluating her own experience as a Chicana lesbian brought up in a repressive subculture, one that in its turn is the object of
oppression by the dominant society. While Anzaldúa comes from an experience
of an obviously mixed race background (she is *la prieta*—dark of skin), Moraga, by contrast, can pass as white (*la güera*—fair of skin). Thus for Moraga, in
contrast to Anzaldúa, the struggle often shapes itself symbolically as an effort
to come to terms with her ability to pass, and her fear of passing.

Loving in the War Years fundamentally concerns itself with the search for her
brown mother and all that search implies: the acknowledgment of her lesbian
identity, the yearning for her lost mother tongue, the desire for her mother's
culture (and her mother's body), the worry about being accepted as a *mestiza*.
As the subtitle of the book suggests, the central image for all of these issues
is that of the mouth, and of the silencing of the Chicana's voice (*lo que nunca
pasó por sus labios*). In *Loving in the War Years* Moraga critiques fellow Chicana
feminists who ignore the contributions of the women's movement, and she
decries homophobia wherever it manifests itself: in the Chicano movement,
among fellow feminist colleagues, and in Chicano culture in general. Thus, for
example, she points out the damage done when sexist Chicano men put down
assertive women by accusing them of lesbianism (similar charges on the part
of Latin American men have poisoned relations with their activist colleagues),
and she highlights the even worse damage suffered when the Chicana leader's
response is merely to deny the accusation. Such responses, she notes, "make
no value judgment on the inherent homophobia in such a divisive tactic. Without comment, her statement reinforces the idea that lesbianism is not only

a white thing, but an insult to be avoided at all costs" (p. 32). Moraga is always attentive to these complex crossings of race and gender politics and the implicit hierarchies of value that they imperfectly uncover. She notes: "It is far easier for the Chicana to criticize white women who on the face of things could never be *familia*, than to take issue with or complain, as it were, to a brother, uncle, father" (pp. 106–107), and she points out the irony of Chicana critics who see no conflict in citing white men like Marx and Engels but ferociously attack fellow Chicanas who find something useful to build upon in feminist theory authored by white women.

In her introduction to her 1993 collection of essays, autobiographical meditations, and poems, *The Last Generation*, Moraga describes the project as "a prayer [written] at a time when I no longer remember how to pray" (p. 1). In keeping with the metaphor of the book as prayer, she frequently evokes language that reminds the reader of its rich religious underpinning. She calls it, for example, a "prophecy" and speaks of "resurrection"; she describes the elegiac quality in terms of the Aztec tradition of "floricanto." There is a particular urgency to this text, a sense of imminent loss. This loss is mostly defined in terms of a gradual abandonment of Mexican culture and traditions:

> I write it against time, out of a sense of urgency that Chicanos are a disappearing tribe, out of sense of this disappearance in my own *familia*. . . . My tíos' children have not taught their own children to be Mexicans. They have become "Americans." And we're all supposed to quietly accept this passing, this slow and painless death of a cultura. . . . But I do not accept it. (p. 2)

In a larger sense, though, the loss is planetary, as Moraga links the fading of Chicano and Native American cultures to the dominant culture's indifference to the environment. The work is divided into five sections, which as a group give a good sense of the book's overall argument: "New Mexican Confessions," "War Cry," "La fuerza femenina," "The Breakdown of the Bicultural Mind," and "The Last Generation."

Much of the book concerns itself with a parsing out of Moraga's own struggles as a light-skinned lesbian Chicana. Born of a Mexican mother and a poor white father, Moraga grew up in a family that prized acculturation; her own turn to the Mexican half of her heritage seemed a betrayal to those family expectations, and coming out as a lesbian seemed strangely to confirm her rebelliousness, as if the terms "Chicana" and "lesbian" somehow support and describe each other by definition. While Moraga can (and at certain periods of her life, did) pass for white, her emotional and intellectual commitment in her adult years has been to her Chicano heritage, and she notes that she holds the customs of her mother's family more dearly because she exercised that choice: "Had I been a full-blood Mexican, I sometimes wonder whether I would have struggled so hard to stay a part of la raza" (p. 127). And yet, this decision is not entirely comprehensible even to her Mexican mother. Moraga's lovely poem, "Credo," begins "frente al altar de mi madre," and in this meeting of mothers, the poetic persona comments: "*Tenemos el mismo problem* / the one says to the other / sin saber the meaning" (p. 65). Here, it is precisely the split across two cultures, two languages, two spiritual systems that causes words to splinter into a poignant incomprehensibility. As Moraga says elsewhere in this volume, naming her pain: "I am always hungry and always shamed by my hunger for the Mexican woman I miss in myself" (p. 121). At the same time, "Credo," the Latin word for "I believe," also echoes with the resonances of the Roman Catholic tradition of her Mexican mother. It is an expression of faith anchored in "this templo / my body" (p. 66).

Like the other Chicana theorists discussed in this article, Moraga also mines Aztec myth for its symbolic system. "Credo," ultimately, is not a Christian poem, but one much closer to the *floricanto* tradition. Moraga also derives her central metaphorical image from one of the goddesses in the Aztec pantheon, in this case, the moon goddess Coyolxauhqui, daughter of Coatlicue and sister of the murderous younger war god Huitzilopochtli. In the myth Huitzilopochtli puts down the rebellion of his older sister, chops her into bits and throws her dismembered body from the top of the pyramid. In Moraga's eloquent description: "Breast splits from chest splits from hip splits from thigh from knee from arm from foot. Coyolxauhqui is banished to the darkness and becomes the moon, *la diosa de la luna*. In my own art, I am writing that wound" (p. 73). She adds a bit later: "Huitzilopotchli is not my god. And although I revere his mother, Coatlicue, Diosa de la Muerte y La Vida, I do not pray to her. I pray to the daughter, La Hija Rebelde. She who has been banished, the mutilated sister who transforms herself into the moon. She is la fuerza femenina" (p. 74). The image of Coyolxauhqui helps Moraga define her own fragmented self, split across competing allegiances of *familia* and family, her two cultures and two bloods. This recognition of fragmentation and a rebellious search for wholeness defines not only her autobiography, but also her writing in general. Moraga notes that all her work focuses on disfigured women and broken men and that her hope is to find, or construct, a whole woman, a free citizen.

Continuing the indigenous metaphor, Moraga ends this book with a piece called "Codex Xerí," which she describes as a "Chicana codex. I offer it as a closing prayer for the last generation" (*The Last Generation*, p. 184). This poem in prose serves as what she calls a record of remembering and a demand for retribution in the name of all dispossessed and fragmented peoples. Her text reminds the reader of the long, slow struggle: "The Chicano codex es una peregrinación [is a pilgrimage] to an América unwritten" (p. 187). And it ends on a positive, or at least rebellious, note. In the face of the dissolution that Moraga elsewhere in the book pessimistically sees as given, in this final chapter she inscribes a challenge: "A Mechicana glyph. Con Safos" (p. 188).

"Queer Aztlán: The Re-formation of Chicano Tribe" is the longest and most directly political of the writings in the volume. In this essay, Moraga reminds her reader of the background to the Chicano movement of 1968 and her own disillusionment with movement politics. She comments that because of the off-putting heterosexism and narrowness in the movement's nationalist agenda, she came to her own real politicization not with the movement, which left her out, but the recognition of her lesbianism. Thus, while Moraga mourns to some degree the dissolution of active Chicano movement, she also recognizes that it belongs to a historical moment that is now past and that even at its best it was problematic and insufficiently progressive. Moraga's own proposal involves revitalized and more inclusive, more progressive movement that she calls in this essay "queer Aztlán." Her discussion of this project begins with a critique of "El Plan Espiritual de Aztlán" by Chicana feminists and gay men, urging that "men have to give up their subscription to male superiority" (p. 161). In contrast with the heterosexist Aztlán of the "Plan espiritual," Moraga suggests that queer Aztlán would be the spiritual homeland for Chicanos that would embrace all of its people.

Moraga's queer Aztlán also extends its embrace to all native peoples of the Americas, in a more than metaphorical sense. Thus, while like her Chicana feminist colleagues Moraga makes use of Aztec mythology to help develop a contesting and non-Western, feminist spiritual practice, she is also aware that the Aztec myth, however spiritually relevant, misses the point to some degree for the real, living people of indigenous heritage in the southwest. She defines a longing to return to indigenous roots that has been a hallmark of Chicana theorizing, but also reminds her reader that this longing is often paired with a lack of knowledge about native cultures. Chicanas, she argues, are mostly of southwestern origin, and thus have a "verifiable genealogy" (p. 166) in Apache, Yaqui, Tarahumara, Navajo and other border nations. One of her most urgent calls to action requires Chicanas to find ways of constructing a community that will connect them to the indigenous nations that share their physical geographies "in order to find concrete solutions for the myriad problems confronting us, from the toxic dump sites in our neighborhoods to rape" (p. 166). Here, Moraga brings the book back to one of her most crucial bottom-line considerations. If, on one level, she theorizes about the fragmented self and a longing for wholeness, on the other she is pragmatically committed to a concrete political agenda revolving around land-based struggles, environmental issues, and the effects of NAFTA.

NORMA ALARCÓN

Among Norma Alarcón's most striking services to the intellectual community has been her apparently unconditional willingness to give of herself as an editor of Third Woman Press and as a participant in colloquia, conferences, symposia, and so forth. She has taken part in a truly mind-boggling number of such activities, and has won considerable visibility in the field as a strong, articulate, and inspirational spokesperson for Chicana studies. At the same time, her work represents one of the most theoretically sophisticated approaches in the field. She is best known for a series of articles that bring together U.S. and European theory, especially 1980s so-called high theory and French Feminist theory, and in her analyses she reinscribes these works into the context of Chicana theorizing. Some of her work is necessarily introductory—introducing and surveying a field that was only beginning to impinge upon the consciousness of the establishment—other essays explore in much more abstract and sophisticated ways the theoretical issues that derive from the specificity of Chicana cultural experience. These pieces have helped open up new approaches and have served as the starting point for other related work that is re-imagining and rethinking not only Chicana and Chicano writing, but also to some extent Mexican literary studies as well.

In all her works, Norma Alarcón has been specifically concerned with developing an ideologically responsible theory of culture and of subjectivity that would help define the particularity of the Chicana feminist subject in contradistinction to both the U.S. dominant culture feminist (or more straightforwardly, what is often defined as the kind of feminism that speaks only to white, middle-class women) and, to a lesser extent, the Mexican feminist movement. The way to this new subjectivity, in the first instance, comes through consciousness-raising, and is inspired by such crucial works as *This Bridge Called My Back*. She notes in her essay on that important book that naming one's experience is one first step to a feminist consciousness, but it is not enough. In much of her work she takes on the hard task of a meticulous exploration of the next step—a nuanced and complex philosophical and cultural analysis.

In her 1992 essay, "Cognitive Desires: An Allegory of/for Chicana Critics," she speaks to the invention of the Chicana—what Alarcón calls her "gene(an)alogy" (p. 187)—playing on the Chicana's yearning for roots and on her recognition that this desired history "could only take shape through this fabulous construction," an analogy which is also a history, which is also a fable (*Chicana (W)rites*, p. 187). While this genealogy is based in the feminine line, Alarcón makes thoughtful use of a wide range of thinkers and philosophers to establish her points. In this essay, for example, Alarcón uses Jean-François Lyotard's notion of the "différend," and Gayatri Spivak's understanding of the subaltern to help her think through the location of the Chicana critic with respect to her intellectual cohort. "My contention," she writes, "is that heretofore the Chicana critic has not taken account of her insider/outsider/insider status with respect to multiple discourse structures. . . . To pursue the nexus of intersectionality of the multiple discourse structures . . . is in a sense to come to terms with the modes through which her disappearance is constantly promoted" (p. 187). At stake in this theoretical question is the issue of how and under what circumstances the subaltern speaks. This question, suggests Alarcón, defines the struggle for both actual and imaginary histories; and histories, she argues, determine position within culture and the political economy.

As Alarcón acutely notes with respect to the Mexican/Chicano studies conference scenario that frames this commentary, texts and other cultural products can cross borders much more easily than people, and individuals are much more tightly bound up in political and nationally defined identities than are their works. In the section entitled "Speaking in Tongues: Cursing the Academy," Alarcón offers a fiery indictment of academic politics that all too often take the institutionalized prerogative "to decide where we belong, which may foreclose almost all possibilities for self-propelled inquiry on the part of Chicanas" (p. 193). She describes three options Chicana critics have exercised in the past for cutting through the double bind that alternately views the Chicana scholar as a wonderful resource and as a narcissistically obsessed minority: (1) the "Richard Rodríguez" option of denying his relationship to his ethnic group while simultaneously affirming it in an oversimplified but coherent story; (2) the orthodox Marxist option of appealing to the generic class struggle; and (3) the resource option often decried as essentializing. In response to these unsatisfactory choices, Alarcón proposes subjects-in-process "who construct provisional (self-determining) 'identities' that subsume a network of discursive and signifying practices and experiences imbricated in the historical *and* imaginary shifting national borders of Mexico and the United States" (p. 198). Alarcón here is very close to the kind of proposal made by Argentine-American philosopher María Lugones when she posits that love (and acceptance of plurality) is central to women-of-color feminisms. For Lugones, Latinas express this love in learning to travel among many different social and psychic worlds, inhabiting more than one mental space at the same time.

One of the places that Alarcón mines for these historical/imaginary identities is Mexican myth. Her much reprinted article "De la literatura feminista de la chicana: Una revisión a través de Malintzin, o Malintzin: Devolver la carne al objeto" is an excellent case in point. In this essay, Alarcón reviews the historical documents describing the original indigenous translator for Hernán Cortés; explores the traditional and highly negative uses of the term *malinchista* in Mexican and Chicano popular culture; and, finally, in her most important contribution, re-evaluates the relevance of this figure in a reimagined, positive framework as an important symbolic image in Chicana feminist writing. Similarly, her more recent article, "Chicana Feminism: In the Tracks of 'The' Native Woman," highlights the reappropriation of a symbolic structure designed around the abstract native Mexican woman, drawing heavily from texts like the *Mitología nahuátl* for inspiration from figures like the Nahua/Aztec goddesses Coatlicue, Cihuacoátl, and Ixtacihuátl. The point, says Alarcón, is not to pretend to recover a lost origin, or a true essence, but rather to define a spiritual kinship with the indigenous part of the Chicana's mestiza heritage; it too is a gene(an)alogy rather than a conventional history or family tree. This claim represents, thus, a pivotal psychic, cultural, and political project. Alarcón compares this project to the U.S. dominant culture concept of the melting pot as an ideological structure and as a "regulative psychobiography" (p. 379). In the melting pot, it is whiteness rather than *mestizaje* that defines the outcome; for the Chicana, the figures of the goddesses, along with other powerful women like Guadalupe, Malinche, and La Llorona, counter U.S. dominant culture models. At the same time and on another level, they also provide a resistant corrective to Mexican dominant culture with its persistent downplaying of the figure of the feminine. Thus, the continuum of meanings constructed in such symbolic gene(an)alogies allows the Chicana to bring the triad of race/class/gender into fruitful discussion, and also opens up "negotiating points . . . to enable 'Chicanas' to grasp their 'I' and 'We' in order to make effective political interventions" (*Living Chicana Theory*, p. 379). Overall, Alarcón's work may sometimes seem very dense and difficult, and perhaps overly reliant on European philosophical structures that in other terms, and on sound ideological ground, she will reject or decry. Nevertheless, she represents some of the best and most powerful abstract thought in the field.

CHELA SANDOVAL

Chela Sandoval also has been thinking through the theoretical implications involved in questions of how to understand women-of-color feminisms in the U.S. context, and this questioning has led to her most important work—densely argued theoretical pieces (her 2000 book, *Methodology of the Oppressed*, offers the most important example, as well as a welcome synthesis of her earlier theoretical work, all of which has led directly to this project) and brief passionate manifestos (such as the frequently reprinted 1981 report on the National Women's Studies Association conference in Oakland). There are several persistent foci of interest in Chela Sandoval's work. Like Alarcón, she is profoundly interested in the complex imbrication of national discourse and literary-theoretical representations, and is especially concerned with the creation and theoretical elaboration of what she calls a "differential" or "oppositional" consciousness among the communities she designates as "U.S. third world feminist critics." She is deeply committed to laying out the history and current strategies of such practices in a rational and coherent form and for this reason her work is frequently structured around well-considered sets of numbered points. Unsurprisingly, her favored vocabulary includes words like "map," "system," "methodology," and "technology," all of which point toward a particularly synthetic structure of mind.

The guiding spirits of Sandoval's *Methodology of the Oppressed* are Jameson, Barthes, and Fanon, and to a lesser extent, her colleagues like Ruth Frankenberg and mentors such as Hayden White and Donna Haraway at the University of California–Santa Cruz (surprisingly, not Paolo Freire, despite the homage to the influential Brazilian thinker in her title). The "methodology" of the title can take various forms—womanism, nomadic consciousness, the mobilization of "love" as a critical category—all of which serve as techniques for the marginalized person to resist and respond to dominant culture practices. The author moves with confidence among some of the most difficult and prickly theorists on the Anglo-French scene. She indicates early in the introduction that she intends this project as an "archeological" analysis of theory, one in which she is as interested in revealing the theorists' unstated hopes and desires as she is in parsing often obscure prose. The body of the book offers fine and trenchant readings of Jameson, Fanon, and Barthes, especially in terms of the unhappy set of cultural and personal circumstances that ultimately prevent these fine thinkers from superseding the paradoxes of their irremediable insertion in the dominant culture. By rereading these classic texts from the point of view of a post-deconstructionist theory of the oppressed, Sandoval rejuvenates these works and offers a fresh and original perspective on them. If she sometimes overstates her case—as in her repeated statement that theory superstar and ultrapopular thinker Roland Barthes "was left alone, abandoned, and in despair" because of his inability to enact a methodology of the repressed—such lapses fade into insignificance alongside the magnitude of this book's achievement and the passion of its argument.

A quite different aspect of Sandoval's work surfaces in the report on the NWSA conference that she wrote while serving as secretary for the National

Third World Women's Alliance. "Feminism and Racism: A Report on the 1981 National Women's Studies Association Conference," like Alarcón's commentary on the 1989 Tijuana conference, describes not only the dynamics of a particular event, but, more importantly, it signals a crucial turning point in Chicana/feminist/third world women's thinking. It is for this reason, more than for its unique historical interest, that the essay has been so frequently reprinted. Sandoval begins her article by echoing Audre Lorde's question, "Do the women of the Academy really *want* to confront racism?" (*Making Face, Making Soul*, p. 56) and anticipates her conclusion by noting, sadly, that the academy apparently preferred no confrontations at all, creating a watered-down version of a liberatory rhetoric instead of opportunities for dialogue. Instead of rich discussion, Sandoval observes a "flamboyant disguise of over-abundance" that created a shopping mall effect (p. 58). At the same time, she says, the very structure of the conference made it "too easy for us to identify who our friends and who our enemies might be. Though empowered as a unity of women of color, the cost is that we find it easy to objectify the occupants of every other category" (p. 65). Finally, she concludes, "through the compassionate inclusion of our differences and the self-conscious understanding that each difference is valid in its context, we are awakened to a new realm of methodological, theoretical, political, and feminist activity" (p. 67), with the potential to reshape the academic field of women's studies. Unfortunately, concrete efforts in that direction met with institutional resistance on the part of some of the white women, and antagonism in both groups. While this antagonism could perhaps be explained away as an unfortunate side effect of a specific organizational mistake, the conclusions Sandoval draws and the implications for institutional theory building have been found valid and important in discussions of the dynamics of women's studies programs as well as other programmatic, departmental, and curricular initiatives.

Alarcón and Sandoval both highlight the slippages in Chicana representations, and Tey Diana Rebolledo, among others, has observed how typical, and how problematic, is this theoretical move: "While Chicana writers were trying to seize their own voices and become speaking subjects, they were at the same time 'decentered' and tended to dissolve into the collective and political. . . . Unable to completely unify or ally with one group, Chicanas felt themselves pulled and pushed (and often rejected) by the various representations" (*Women Singing in the Snow*, p. 102). This is an equivocal positioning at best, since, as José Esteban Muñoz reminds us, all too frequently the "discourses of essentialism and constructivism short circuit" (*Disidentifications: Queers of Color and the Performance of Politics*, p. 6). For minority subjects, the effort to resist dominant ideology is fraught with peril and, in these writers, often expressed in prose that seems fiendishly complex.

ANA CASTILLO

Like the writings of her colleagues and collaborators Gloria Anzaldúa and Cherríe Moraga, Ana Castillo's *Massacre of the Dreamers: Essays in Xicanisma* (1994) deeply influenced the U.S. third world women's movement. Ana Castillo is from Chicago, thus adding the midwestern United States to the map created by this essential triad of feminist thinkers, and complementing Anzaldúa's Texas-based border theory and Moraga's California. Castillo begins her book with a discussion of the roots of *machismo*, tracing it back to the preconquest Arab heritage in Spanish culture. She then explores the intersection of Roman Catholic liberation theology and feminist spirituality, in counterpoint to the male-dominated Chicano movement and its roots in a more conservative version of Catholicism, despite claims deriving from its leftist rhetoric. The next three chapters of the book, "In the Beginning There Was Eva," "La Macha: Toward an Erotic Whole Self," and "Brujas and Curanderas: A Lived Spirituality," serve as the analogous chapters to the central section of Anzaldúa's *Borderlands/La Frontera*. In this section, Castillo, like Anzaldúa, works on elaborating an alternative, feminocentric spirituality with broad implications for feminist practice. Her concept of Xicanisma implicitly contrasts with Chicanismo, which Castillo would see as overly contaminated by *machismo*, and hence unsalvageable in any real sense by the feminist of color. Thus, the Xicanista, and Xicanismo in general, serve an analogous function to Anzaldúa's Coatlicue state, though Castillo grounds her project more straightforwardly in a conception of the woman's body that is distinctly maternal. In each case, the most prized quality for the writer is a sense of community among whole, empowered women who are claiming their rights to full participation in their societies. This community naturally and essentially evolves as a spiritual one, as, says Castillo, "women's history is one of religiosity" (*Massacre of the Dreamers*, p. 145). In tracing this heritage, Castillo finds significant links among U.S. indigenous American, African (Yoruba), and Aztec customs that confirm her faith in the strength of traditional healing practices and suggest to her their relevance in a woman's path to self-empowerment. In support of this argument, Castillo confirms her credentials as the granddaughter of a *curandera*, and even offers her own recipe for an herbal bath "to cleanse the self of negative energies in the environment, to rid one of an unsettling feeling, or regularly, for chronic anxiety" (p. 160).

The heart of the project is "Un Tapiz: The Poetics of Conscientización." Significantly, Castillo calls this section a poetics rather than a theory, and the distinction is an important one. Like her colleagues Moraga and Anzaldúa, Castillo is a poet, and while this book is less of an obviously mixed-genre production than that of the other two writers, her sensibility is equally a poetic one. Like theirs, her form of argumentation accordingly builds upon a metaphorical and lyrical logic that does not match the traditional Western style of proof. Castillo writes: "The vast majority of us were taught to be afraid of a certain type of English: the language of Anglos who initiated and sustained our social and economic disenfranchisement. . . . At the same time, we were equally intimidated by the Spanish spoken by people of middle-class or higher economic strata who came from Latin America" (p. 167). She is, then, concerned with the way language shapes reality and forms (or deforms) community. Castillo urges her Xicanista readers to face these fears and to take responsibility for their many languages—to hold themselves accountable for their use. In taking charge of the ideas they communicate, the Xicanistas "may begin to introduce unimaginable images and concepts into our poetics" (p. 170). This is what Castillo calls, finally, a "conscienticized poetics" (p. 171), using a loan-blend from the Spanish language in the absence of an adequate English word.

Castillo's "tapiz" highlights three works: Anzaldúa's *Borderlands/La Frontera*, Moraga's *Loving in the War Years*, and her own novel, *The Mixquiahuala Letters*. Castillo contrasts the former two works as follows: "Anzaldúa's spiritual affinity for Coatlicue serves as a resonant reflection of her desire for disembodiment that would free her from a tremendous physical and emotional anguish. . . . Moraga . . . contrary to Anzaldúa's *Borderlands*, reflects an acute connection with her physical self and sexuality" (p. 173). She later adds: "While Anzaldúa would have us see her physical self as indistinguishable from her spiritual image of duality, Moraga concludes the opposite, that is, she claims the spiritual through the physical" (pp. 176–177). For her own part, Castillo describes her novel as an example of "public risk-taking" and notes that "the ideological problem that the personal is political does not include a formal, theoretical solution" (p. 179). Her character, Teresa, is a subversive, insurgent, feminist woman analogous to the central figures in the narratives of her counterparts. All three women, then, in form and content of their work embody a similar ethics: "Subversion of all implied truths is necessary in order to understand the milieu of sexist politics that shape the lives of women" (p. 177). At moments like these, Castillo's urgency may make her voice seem a bit too strident, a bit too categorical, a bit too close to the twinned evils of white oppression and Chicano movement politics for which it explicitly serves as a countervoice and counternarrative.

And yet, Ana Castillo's manifesto-like conclusion to *Massacre of the Dreamers* calls for a resurrection in terms as purely lyrical as anything we have seen from any of the writers surveyed here. These words, this call to action, serve as a conclusion to this piece as well:

What we have been permitted to be without argument in society is the compassionate, cooperative, yielding, procreator of the species, india fea, burra beast of burden of society. Viewed as ugly and common as straw. We know that we are not. Let us be alchemists for our culture and our lives and use this conditioning as our raw material to convert it into a driving force pure as gold. (p. 226)

SELECTED BIBLIOGRAPHY

Alarcón, Norma. "Chicana Feminism: In the Tracks of 'The' Native Woman." In *Living Chicana Theory*. Edited by Carla Trujillo. Berkeley, Calif.: Third Woman Press, 1998. Pp. 371–382.

———. "Cognitive Desires: An Allegory of/for Chicana Critics." In *Chicana (W)rites: On Word and Film*. Edited by Maria Herrera-Sobek and Helena Maria Viramontes. Berkeley, Calif.: Third Woman Press, 1995. Pp. 185–200.

———. "De la literatura feminista de la chicana: Una revisión a través de Malintzin, o Malintzin: Devolver la carne al objeto." In *Esta puente mi espalda: Voces de mujeres tercer mundistas en los Estados Unidos.* Edited by Cherríe Moraga and Ana Castillo. San Francisco, Calif.: Ism Press, 1988. Pp. 231–241.

———. "The Theoretical Subject(s) of *This Bridge Called My Back* and Anglo-American Feminism." In *Making Face, Making Soul/Haciendo caras: Creative and Critical Perspectives by Feminists of Color.* Edited by Gloria Anzaldúa. San Francisco, Calif.: Spinsters/ Aunt Lute Books, 1990. Pp. 356–369.

———. "Traddutora, Traditora: A Paradigmatic Figure of Chicana Feminism." *Cultural Critique,* vol. 13 (fall 1989): 57–87.

Alarcón, Norma, Ana Castillo, and Cherríe Moraga, eds. *Third Woman: Sexuality of Latinas.* Berkeley, Calif.: Third Woman Press, 1993.

Anzaldúa, Gloria. *Borderlands/La Frontera: The New Mestiza.* San Francisco, Calif.: Spinsters/ Aunt Lute Books, 1987.

———. "En Rapport, In Opposition: Cobrando cuentas a las nuestras." In *Making Face, Making Soul/Haciendo caras: Creative and Critical Perspectives by Feminists of Color.* Edited by Gloria Anzaldúa. San Francisco, Calif.: Spinsters/Aunt Lute Books, 1990. Pp. 142–148.

———, ed. *Making Face, Making Soul/Haciendo caras: Creative and Critical Perspectives by Feminists of Color.* San Francisco, Calif.: Spinsters/Aunt Lute Books, 1990.

Castillo, Ana. *Massacre of the Dreamers: Essays on Xicanisma.* Albuquerque: University of New Mexico Press, 1994.

Castillo, Debra, and María Socorro Tabuenca Córdoba. *Border Women: Writing from La Frontera.* Minneapolis: University of Minnesota Press, 2002.

Chabram-Dernersesian, Angie. "I Throw Punches for My Race, but I Don't Want to Be a Man: Writing Us—Chica-nos (Girl, Us)/Chicanas—into the Movement Script." In *Cultural Studies: A Critical Reader.* Edited by Lawrence Grossberg, Cary Nelson, and Paula Treichler. New York: Routledge, 1992. Pp. 81–95.

Cota-Cárdenas, Margarita. "Manifestación tardía." *La Palabra,* vol. 2, no. 2 (1980).

del Castillo, Adelaida. "Mexican Women in Organization." In *Mexican Women in the United States.* Edited by Magdalena Mora and Adelaida del Castillo. Los Angeles: Chicano Studies Center, 1980. Pp. 7–16.

Garcia, Alma. *Chicana Feminist Thought: The Basic Historical Writings.* New York: Routledge, 1977.

Herrera-Sobek, Maria, and Helena Maria Viramontes, eds. *Chicana Creativity and Criticism: Charting New Frontiers in American Literature.* Albuquerque: University of New Mexico Press, 1996.

———. *Chicana (W)rites: On Word and Film.* Berkeley, Calif.: Third Woman Press, 1995.

Hurtado, Aida. *The Color of Privilege: Three Blasphemies on Race and Feminism.* Ann Arbor: University of Michigan Press, 1996.

———. *Voicing Chicana Feminisms: Young Women Speak Out on Sexuality and Identity.* New York: New York University Press, 2003.

Lugones, María. "Playfulness, 'World'–Traveling, and Loving Perception." In *Making Face, Making Soul/Haciendo caras: Creative and Critical Perspectives by Feminists of Color.* Edited by Gloria Anzaldúa. San Francisco, Calif.: Spinsters/Aunt Lute Books, 1990. Pp. 390–402.

Michaelsen, Scott, and David E. Johnson, eds. *Border Theory: The Limits of Cultural Politics.* Minneapolis: University of Minnesota Press, 1997.

Mignolo, Walter D. *Local Histories/Global Designs: Coloniality, Subaltern Knowledges, and Border Thinking.* Princeton, N.J.: Princeton University Press, 2000.

———. "Posoccidentalismo: El argumento desde América Latina." *Cuadernos americanos,* vol. 12, no. 67 (1998): 143–165.

Mora, Pat. *Nepantla: Essays from the Land in the Middle.* Albuquerque: University of New Mexico Press, 1993.

Moraga, Cherríe. *Giving up the Ghost: Teatro in Two Acts.* Los Angeles, Calif.: West End Press, 1986.

———. *The Last Generation.* Boston, Mass.: South End Press, 1993.

———. *Loving in the War Years: Lo que nunca pasó por sus labios.* Boston, Mass.: South End Press, 1983.

Moraga, Cherríe, and Gloria Anzaldúa, eds. *This Bridge Called My Back.* Watertown, Mass.: Persephone Press, 1981.

Moraga, Cherríe, and Ana Castillo, eds. *Esta puente mi espalda: Voces de mujeres tercer mundistas en los Estados Unidos.* San Francisco, Calif.: Ism Press, 1988.

Muñoz, José Esteban. *Disidentifications: Queers of Color and the Performance of Politics.* Minneapolis: University of Minnesota Press, 1999.

Quintana, Alvina. "Politics, Representation, and the Emergence of a Chicana Aesthetics." *Cultural Studies,* vol. 4 (1990): 72–83.

Rebolledo, Tey Diana. *Women Singing in the Snow: A Cultural Analysis of Chicana Literature.* Tucson: University of Arizona Press, 1995.

Rendón, Armando. *The Chicano Manifesto.* New York: Macmillan, 1971.

Saenz, Benjamin Alire. "In the Borderlands of Chicano Identity, There Are Only Fragments." In *Border Theory: The Limits of Cultural Politics.* Edited by Scott Michaelsen and David E. Johnson. Minneapolis: University of Minnesota Press, 1997. Pp. 68–96.

Saldívar-Hull, Sonia. *Feminism on the Border: Chicana Gender Politics and Literature.* Berkeley: University of California Press, 2000.

Sánchez, Rosaura, and Rosa Martínez Cruz. *Essays on la mujer.* Los Angeles: Chicano Studies Center Publications, University of California, 1977.

Sandoval, Chela. "Feminism and Racism: A Report on the 1981 National Women's Studies Association Conference." In *Making Face, Making Soul/Haciendo caras: Creative and Critical Perspectives by Feminists of Color.* Edited by Gloria Anzaldúa. San Francisco, Calif.: Spinsters/Aunt Lute Books, 1990. Pp. 55–71.

———. "Mestizaje as Method: Feminists-of-Color Challenge the Canon." In *Living Chicana Theory.* Edited by Carla Trujillo. Berkeley, Calif.: Third Woman Press, 1988. Pp. 352–370.

———. *Methodology of the Oppressed.* Minneapolis: University of Minnesota Press, 2000.

Tabuenca Córdoba, María-Socorro. "Viewing the Border: Perspectives from 'the Open Wound.'" *Discourse,* vol. 18, no. 1–2 (1995–1996): 146–168.

Tafolla, Carmen. *To Split a Human: Mitos, machos, y la mujer Chicana.* San Antonio, Tex.: Mexican American Cultural Center, 1985.

Trujillo, Carla, ed. *Chicana Lesbians: The Girls Our Mothers Warned Us About.* Berkeley, Calif.: Third Woman Press, 1991.

———, ed. *Living Chicana Theory.* Berkeley, Calif.: Third Woman Press, 1998.

"What Doesn't Kill You, Makes You Fat": The Language of Food in Latina Literature

Jacqueline Zeff

From Mrs. Shimerda's gift of mysterious mushrooms in *My Ántonia* to Pat Mora's life "in a doorway/between two rooms"—one serving black coffee and the other café con leche, American women writers have spoken to their readers through the language of food. Esmeralda Santiago begins her first memoir, *When I Was Puerto Rican*, with a prologue on "How to Eat a Guava."* She is at the Shop & Save in New York City, and as she fingers a green guava its smell transports her to the ripe yellow guava memories of Puerto Rico. "If you don't know how to eat a guava," she warns,

> the seeds end up in the crevices between your teeth. When you bite into a ripe guava, your teeth must grip the bumpy surface and sink into the thick edible skin without hitting the center. It takes experience to do this. . . . (3)

She also recalls the hard, unripe guava of her childhood when impatience and daring could not wait: "You hear the skin, meat, and seeds crunching inside your head, while the inside of your mouth explodes in little spurts of sour." But she pushes her shopping cart away from the fruit of her youth and toward the apples and pears of adulthood with "their nearly seedless ripeness predictable and bittersweet" (4). To be sure, such a bittersweet experience of loss is a common feature in the literature of first generation Americans; and the use of the senses to carry the burden of childhood is familiar to readers of American ethnic literatures. But in the fiction and poetry of several Latina writers, food—its preparation, consumption, sensuality, and power—carries more than the memory of home; food is not only the message but the medium of love, the spirit, survival, even art itself.

Reproduced with permission from Jacqueline Zeff, "'What Doesn't Kill You, Makes You Fat': The Language of Food in Latina Literature," in the *Journal of American Culture* (v25.i1–2: pp. 94–99).

In *Peel My Love Like an Onion* by Ana Castillo, the protagonist Carmen Santos recalls her first amorous encounter with Manolo, the great love of her life. "When you are in love," asserts Carmen at the very start of the novel, "no single metaphor is enough" (1). Castillo certainly never runs out of them, but the first consummation for Carmen and Manolo relies on images of food:

> He brought me close to him between his legs, me still standing, pulled my face down to his to kiss me. Then, in one quick movement, my undergarments were gone and my skirt was up over my head and he had me spread before him like a Sunday brunch buffet. Not a position I objected to at all. . . . (81)

Carmen describes her lover's youth and appearance:

> Mi Manolío was dark, even in winter, his skin savory and sweet like Mexican chocolate that makes your mouth water just to whiff it simmering and waiting for you on the stove to have with your birthday cake. Manolo was a birthday cake with exactly twenty lit candles when we met. A cake not quite done yet. And I was the birthday girl surprised in the dark. (83)

The narrator of Kathleen Alcalá's short story, "The Transforming Eye," is also in for quite a surprise when she comes to Los Picos, a small Mexican town, to help her grandmother, Abuelita Clara, die. The narrator resembles her grandmother "with our high cheekbones and curly hair" (3) but they will share much more than that by story's end. In her walks through the town's plaza, the narrator discovers what seems a photographer's shop or artist's studio as her two "ancient" great-aunts describe it. The shop "sagged with dust and neglect" (5) but the narrator strikes up a friendship with the original owner's son, despite her aunts' warnings that his father was "involved in sorcery, or some such trash" (7). The narrator is especially drawn to a beautiful painted backdrop, Moorish and lush with flowers and trees. And in the center, "two lime-green parrots shared a hoop and touched bills affectionately, framed by a full moon" (6). The store owner's son repairs the old camera and invites the narrator to sit before the backdrop, because to tell if the camera works, he needs a human subject. As he gazes at her through the lens and exposes the plate he comments on her beautiful eyes that remind him of a woman his father knew.

When the narrator returns to the empty shop several days later she finds some newly hand tinted prints on the counter:

> They showed a serious young woman holding a bowl of pomegranates in her lap . . . I admired the life-like quality of the photos, until I realized that the woman in the picture was me. (11)

Or someone like her. She moves deeper into the studio and is lured to the backdrop at which point the mystery and metaphor confound surface reality, for

on the stone bench in the scene was a wooden bowl full of deliciously
red pomegranates. They looked so real that I couldn't restrain myself
from reaching to pick one up. The leathery skin and prickly end felt as
real to me as any fruit I had ever touched. I turned with the pomegranate in my hand and saw that I stood on the black and white tiles, the
bright trees trailing their branches over my head. The photographer's
studio appeared vague and dim, as though seen through a gauze cur-
tain. I was inside the backdrop. (12)

In the backdrop she finds her grandmother's handkerchief. With all the power
of nightmare, the narrator screams and claws to free herself, sometimes seeing visions and hearing birds singing. The claustrophobic horror of the vision
evokes the psychological confinement of the women of Los Picos, but then the
narrator acts: "I ate two of the pomegranates" (13). In this Eden, Eve is freed—
not punished—for tasting the tree of knowledge. And it is finally the coming
of her grandmother into the nightmare, in search of the man she loves, who
frees the granddaughter from the backdrop. She returns to her great-aunts'
house to learn that her grandmother has died. The story concludes with an insistence on the reality of the vision, for as the narrator leaves Los Picos forever,
she takes the lesson of the pomegranates with her: "I hid my battered finger-
nails in my grandmother's handkerchief and refused to look back again" (15).
In this strange and wonderful tale, a woman eats her way to freedom and to a
bond of love that transcends the generations.

   Food in Latina literature is also, to use Doris Friedensohn's term, "a yard-
stick of consciousness" that reflects the tensions between the multiple identities bestowed on us by others and those views of the self we construct for
ourselves (165). In her essay, "Chapulines, Mole and Pozole: Mexican Cuisines and the Gringa Imagination," Friedensohn recounts her own journey
as a gastronomic "tourist" noting that "writing about food is primal and
confrontational—like looking in the mirror or arguing with a lover" (166). She
celebrates her triumph over chapolines, the distinctly Oaxacan dish of fried
grasshoppers, tastes the irony of eating traditional mole negro in a decidedly
untraditional tourist restaurant, and manages to consume two pozoles in one
day. She embraces a multicultural commitment to eating as a way of literally
and emotionally broadening her identity. But Freidensohn has only eaten her
way through the outermost layers of the onion: "there are such deep and elaborate constructions of the self to confront, so many real and imagined barriers
to overcome" (174). One of the essential barriers in much of women's literature
is that between the embodied self and the embodied spirit. For Latina writers,
food seems to be a more available passageway through that barrier than, say,
a bell jar, a room of one's own, or a mother's garden.

   Julia Alvarez published her first book, a collection of poems called *Homecoming*, in 1984. Twelve years later she reissued the collection with several
new poems and a new sonnet sequence. In an Afterword to the new collection,
Alvarez notes how she now sees "how fiercely I was claiming my woman's
voice" (119). In an early poem in the collection, "What could it be?" Alvarez
listens to that voice take shape in the kitchen: "Around the kettle of chicken

and rice/the aunts were debating what flavor was missing." Garlic? Pepper? Plain salt? Until Tía Victoria insists on tarragon. Then the aunts all join in a frenzy of seasoning, each putting in "a shake of their favorites." This commingling of individual preferences is given the powerful image it deserves as the women "cackled like witches, sampled, and nodded" while "The uncles ate seconds and rose in a chorus/of chair scrapes and belches . . ." (29). The older, more confident Alvarez has spiced up her own sense of self in this new edition, adding a few Spanish terms of connection such as tía which were absent from the first edition. Alvarez concedes the tentative self such omissions reveal:

> Except for "Homecoming," the poem that opened the original book, I did not address my experience as a Dominican-American woman. Indeed, that earlier voice did not even feel permission to do so, as if to call attention to my foreignness would make my readers question my right to write in English. (119)

The men in the poem remain "uncles" but the women who cook have helped her reconcile her English self with her Spanish spirit.

In the novel *Mother Tongue* by Demetria Martínez, Mary—or María as her El Salvadorean refugee lover re-names her—is urged by her mentor, Soledad, to eat her way back to mental health. At nineteen, María "was looking for a man to tear apart the dry rind" of her identity "so I could see what fruit fermented inside" (16). But when her lover resists her wish to marry and forget his troubled homeland, Mary—now María—despairs. Soledad advises her in a letter. "Food is the best medicine," she writes to María,

> All this depression going around—it's because we've gotten too far away from the foods of our ancestors. And our cells never forget. . . . We must make every effort to eat what our elders ate, eat with the seasons, and eat what is grown nearby. (110)

Benay Blend argues in her essay, " 'In the Kitchen Family Bread Is Always Rising!'—Women's Culture and the Politics of Food," that to embrace the kitchen—and the preparation and consumption of food—is one way women writers reconcile the tensions between an authentic self and the domestic role for women that works against the development of that self. Demetria Martínez probably agrees with Blend's argument, for she not only includes Soledad's letters of advice on men and faith and politics, but has María insert Soledad's recipe for posole into the story. Its placement is important: it appears between examples of Soledad's political activism on behalf of the underground and her advice on how to resist men from taking over one's self. Since falling in love is "a socially acceptable way for a woman to be insane" (27) Martínez is suggesting perhaps that the way to preserve the self from that insanity is to believe in a cause beyond the self. Even if that cause is posole. "You'd be amazed at how learning to cook takes your mind off men," writes Soledad "—if you do it for your own pleasure. Why do you think I'm such a good cook?" (117).

In her discussion of Pat Mora's memoir, *House of Houses*, Blend describes another reason to seek such "medicine." She interprets Mora's craving for recipes as a way to identify with female ancestors:

> Recollecting family lore, she [Mora] evokes a sense of full family life, of the close bonds that in turn produce the narrator herself. She discovers that from the kitchen emanates not only food making but also ritual, tradition, and family history. (149)

Food does even more than heal body and spirit in two very different tributes to love: the romantic fantasy *Like Water for Chocolate* by Laura Esquivel, and a "memoir of the senses," *Aphrodite*, by Isabel Allende. Food saves life itself and becomes a medium for survival—or destruction of life. Indeed, both works rely on narratives of food—what we usually call recipes—for their structure and emotive power. Both carry unusual prologues that establish a language of food to unmask human relationships. *Like Water for Chocolate* begins with an epigram: "To the table or to bed/You must come when you are bid" and *Aphrodite* is dedicated "to playful lovers and, why not? also to frightened men and melancholy women." Esquivel's magical love story is organized around a series of twelve recipes for twelve seasons for twelve chapters. Not only do the recipes figure in the plots of the chapters but they permeate the novel's point of view. Each chapter begins with its own "preparation" and commentary on the list of ingredients that face the first page of each chapter. The narrative voice speaks directly to the reader with instructions and even warnings to ensure a successful end result: "Take care to chop the onion fine" (5); "Remove the petals carefully from the roses, trying not to prick your fingers" (47); "It's advisable to toast the cocoa beans just until the moment they begin to give off oil" (165). In Chapter 2, the star-crossed lover Tita is preparing a wedding cake for her beloved Pedro who is to marry her sister, Rosaura. She has just determined that Pedro in fact loves her and not her sister. Tita's voluminous tears have already threatened the thickening of the cake batter, and when Tita begins the final preparations for the cake's icing her tears prevent the meringue from peaking so Nacha, the cook, sends Tita off to bed and finishes making the frosting herself. She licks her fingers to determine whether all those tears from Tita has diluted the flavor. To Nacha's surprise, the frosting has not been affected "yet, without knowing why, Nacha was suddenly overcome with an intense longing" (36). Later, as the wedding guests consume the cake, they are all similarly affected:

> The moment they took their first bite of the cake, everyone was flooded with a great wave of longing. Even Pedro, usually so proper, was having trouble holding back his tears. (39)

But tears are soon followed by other "symptoms of a strange intoxication" and before long the wedding guests are collectively vomiting all over the patio (39). All, except Tita. Tita's cruelly demented mother is convinced Tita poisoned the cake and beats her so badly that she must spend two weeks in bed recovering. "Tita was never able to convince her," writes Esquivel, "that she had only added one extra ingredient to the cake, the tears she had shed while preparing it" (41). This exquisite albeit fleeting moment of justice for Tita illumines the rich power of food which eludes the imagination of both older women. Nacha can only predict that human tears affect the physical composition of the food while Mama Elena can only conclude that humans need help from the physical world to change human events. They are both wrong, as Tita demonstrates repeatedly in the novel: for example, producing milk from her non-lactating breasts to keep her starving nephew (and Pedro's son) alive. And entering Pedro's body through her quail in rose petal sauce: "hot, voluptuous, perfumed, totally sensuous" (52).

At novel's end, with Tita and Pedro literally consumed in the fires of their love, Tita's great niece has inherited all that remains of the family ranch—the cookbook which "tells in each of its recipes this story of a love interred" (246). The recipes embody Tita and Pedro in a profoundly literal way. And the niece's concluding words in the novel argue for the power of food as narrative. She tells her readers she is preparing Christmas Rolls (the first recipe/chapter in the novel) aware that her great-aunt "will go on living as long as there is some-one who cooks her recipes" (246). And that living is incarnate, not sentimental recollection. Food and women have a reciprocity of feeling that complicates any conventional understanding of "comfort food."

Isabel Allende testifies from her personal experience to the restorative and creative power of food in *Aphrodite*. The book is a compendium of aphrodisia-cal recipes and sensual shopping lists, a history of what Allende describes in her introduction as her "relationship with food and eroticism" (9). The idea for the book originated in that unspeakable experience of a mother grieving for a dying daughter. In 1991, in Madrid, she orders five servings of rice pud-ding, her favorite dessert, and as she recalls,

> ate them down without blinking, with the vague hope that the nostalgic dessert from my childhood would help me bear the anguish of seeing my daughter so ill. . . . After the death of my daughter, Paula, I spent three years trying to exorcise my sadness with futile rituals. (24)

It was not until her first food dream, however, that she knew she had a path to recovery. In January, 1996 Allende dreamed that she jumped into a swim-ming pool filled with rice pudding. Such a dream could only lead one place: "I . . . threw myself on my husband before the poor man realized what was happening to him" (24). Allende understands that food is not simply or mainly a substitute for love (as the current diet advice for women would tell us)—it is a way to conjure the dead and invoke the spirit of life:

> . . . when my dreams about food began, I knew that I was reaching the end of a long tunnel of mourning and finally coming out the other end, into the light, with a tremendous desire to eat and cuddle once again. And so, little by little, pound after pound and kiss after kiss, this project was born. (25)

Just as Esquivel returns to the Christmas Rolls in her final chapter, Allende offers as her final recipe "Arroz con leche, or Spiritual Solace" (315). She "can't imagine a more sensual or delicious dessert" and confesses her capacity for pleasure:

> This recipe will serve eight normal people, but in my eyes it's a crime to make less. I'm capable of devouring it at one sitting without blinking an eye, and I don't see why it should be any different in your case, my dear reader. But if you can't finish, you can keep it in the refrigerator, then, should you be in a good mood, you can cover your lover from head to foot with this mouthwatering arroz con leche and slowly lick it off. On such an occasion the calories are justified. (315)

I think Tita would agree.

Latina writers endow their cooks with one more special role, that of the artist. And as artists do, even the Latina cook can suffer a creative block. For months since declaring her love for Pedro and his for her, Tita has been inventing recipes, hoping to reestablish the link produced by her rose petal sauce.

> Just as a poet plays with words, Tita juggled ingredients and quantities at will, obtaining phenomenal results, and all for nothing: her best efforts were in vain. (64)

She did not know that Mother Elena had "censored" her culinary poetry, prohibiting Pedro from complimenting Tita's cooking. Tita will inevitably connect to Pedro, but this time not so much through her food, but through her own actions as the maker of the food. When Tita is preparing a turkey mole for the baptismal feast for her nephew, Pedro is lured into the kitchen by the smell of almond and sesame seeds toasting on the griddle. But he stops "stock-still" in the doorway to the kitchen: Tita is "on her knees . . . bent over the grinding stone, moving in a slow regular rhythm" (66). Not even Allende could imagine a more erotic moment: Tita's braless breasts "moved freely" and sweat forms on her neck "and ran down into the crease between her firm round breasts" (67). Tita looks up at Pedro and their "passionate glances" fuse "perfectly," even as Tita continues to "grind." Tita heats it up a notch when she straightens and lifts her chest to give Pedro a better look. Pedro's gaze now transforms her breasts "from chaste to experienced flesh, without even touching them" (67). Perhaps poetry is meant to be seen as well as heard!

Allende similarly compares the baking of bread to the making of art:

> Like poetry, baking is a rather melancholy vocation, whose primary requirement is free time for the soul. The poet and the baker are brothers in the essential task of nourishing the world. (127)

In the opening, title poem of *The Latin Deli* Judith Ortiz Cofer makes the link between food and art directly, subtitling the poem "An Ars Poetica." The deli owner, whose history is told later in the collection in the short story "Corazón's

Café," spends her days selling "canned memories" to the Puerto Rican customers who buy homeland brands and native foods and go down the store's aisles reciting package labels aloud "as if/they were the names of lost lovers" (3). Their shopping lists are read aloud to her "like poetry." In the poem "From the Book of Dreams in Spanish" Ortiz Cofer imagines herself feeding on the rich ripe fruit of her homeland but she is left a literally starving artist, cut off from the words that would fill her up. For Meredith Abarca in her essay "Los Chilaquiles de Mi 'Ama: The Language of Everyday Cooking," transforming a recipe—which is made of words, after all—into food is a unique act of the mixing of ingredients with the cook's personal chiste (twist). The artist remakes her recipe in much the same way the poet remakes the ordering and balance and mixture of words.

But just because the cook is an artist, does that make the artist a cook? Julia Alvarez confronts what she calls "the spaghetti in my head" (128) in a courageous essay, "Family Matters," in which she examines the sources of her writing talent and style. She asks—somewhat fearfully—to what extent is her style let alone her subject matter derived from la familia and to what extent from her "working" language, English? She makes some interesting discoveries. An editor who was working with her on a magazine story pointed to her overuse of the word "little"—"A little coffee, a little desert, a little cough." Alvarez learns that she was transferring the common Spanish diminutive of family talk into her English style. She acknowledges her familia storytelling as well with its "bittersweet approach, the heart in turmoil but a twinkle in the eye" (126). In another essay, "Of Maids and Other Muses," Alvarez records her discovery of her true voice and subject, an epiphany many women writers acknowledge when they abandon the misconception that they should be writing about something "important," that to claim authority is to write "about the big matters that Milton, Yeats, Homer had tackled" (147). For Alvarez, as for Paule Marshall, Marge Piercy, Toni Morrison and so many other women writers, that epiphany takes place in the kitchen. But the process and substance of the encounter is distinct and Latina. Alvarez recalls the first time she heard her own voice on paper. She was living for a time at Yaddo and she was in her tower room "waiting for inspiration" (160). It did not come. Yes, she heard the voices of women from the kitchens of her childhood gossiping in her head, but these voices were not for paper. "And then," recalls Alvarez,

> hallelujah—I heard the vacuum going up and down the hall. I opened the door and introduced myself to the friendly, sweating woman, wielding her vacuum cleaner. She invited me down to the kitchen so we wouldn't disturb the other guests. There I met the cook, and as we all sat, drinking coffee, I paged through her old cookbook: knead, poach, stew, whip, score, julienne, whisk, sauté, sift. Hmm. I began hearing a music in these words. I jotted down the names of implements:
>
> Cup, spoon, ladle, pot, kettle,
> grater and peeler,
> colander, corer,
> waffle, iron, small funnel.

> "You working on a poem there?" the cook asked me.
> I shook my head.
> A little later, I went upstairs to the tower room and wrote down in my
> journal this beautiful vocabulary of my girlhood. (161)

So it is only fitting that Alvarez married a man, Bill Eichner, who cooks, and is
the author of the *New Family Cookbook*.

In *A Cafecito Story* (little, again!), Alvarez tells a parable drawn from her
own childhood memories of the traditional, shaded coffee farms in the Dominican Republic and her husband's childhood memories of the technifica-
tion of Nebraska family farms. Together they established an organic coffee
farm foundation in the mountains of the Dominican Republic, called Alta
Gracia. In the parable, Joe (Bill) helps Miguel and other traditional farmers
resist the compañía's plan to rent all the land and cut down the trees, to speed
the coffee planting process and corrupt its taste. But the story is not just economic, for the farmers are also learning to plant ideas in their own minds
and the minds of their children through reading lessons offered by Joe. By
the time Miguel and his wife Carmen and their children have learned to write
their names

> the little seeds have sprouted. When the trees are a foot high, the family
> has struggled through a sentence. All of them can read a page by the
> time the trees reach up to Miguel's knees. . . . [I]n three years, by the time
> of the first coffee harvest from trees Joe has planted, Miguel and Carmen
> and their children can read a whole book. (24–25)

Now the art of writing transfigures the world of nature itself. As Alvarez
notes:

> It is amazing how much better coffee grows when sung to by birds or
> when through an opened window comes the sound of a human voice
> reading words on paper that still holds the memory of the tree it used
> to be. (25)

Our cells never forget . . . nor do nature's, apparently.

The language of food offers the Latina writer a complex vocabulary of empowerment and sensuality, of solitude and resistance. In her second memoir,
Almost a Woman, Esmeralda Santiago gives us a taste of that language through
her mother's allocation of American and Puerto Rican food. It is their first winter in New York City and she and her siblings suffer cold after cold in their un-
heated apartment. Santiago's mother fights back by trying to "thicken" their
Puerto Rican blood with American foods: "Mami gave us canned American
food every day for a week, but our colds didn't disappear with anything but
a spoonful of tutumá" (24). The language of food is indeed a recipe for Latina storytelling and imagery, and the American literary diet is richer for each
spoonful.

NOTE

The title of this article includes one of the proverbial headings in Santiago's memoir.

WORKS CITED

Abarca, Meredith E. "Los Chilaquiles de Mi 'Ama: The Language of Everyday Cooking." *Pilaf, Pozole, and Pad Thai: American Women and Ethnic Food.* Ed. Sherrie A. Inness. Amherst: U of Massachusetts P, 2001. 119–144.

Alcalá, Kathleen. "The Transforming Eye." *Mrs. Vargas and the Dead Naturalist.* Corvallis, OR: Calyx Books, 1992, 1–15.

Allende, Isabel. *Aphrodite: A Memoir of the Senses.* New York: HarperCollins, 1998.

Alvarez, Julia. *A Cafecito Story.* White River Junction, VT: Chelsea Green Publishing, 2001.

——. "Family Matters." *Something to Declare.* New York: Penguin, 1998. 113–129.

——. *Homecoming: New and Collected Poems.* New York: Penguin, 1996.

——. "Of Maids and Other Muses." *Something to Declare.* New York: Penguin, 1998. 147–162.

Blend, Benay. "In the Kitchen Family Bread Is Always Rising! Women's Culture and the Politics of Food." *Pilaf, Pozole, and Pad Thai: American Women and Ethnic Food.* Ed. Sherrie A. Inness. Amherst: U of Massachusetts P, 2001. 145–164.

Castillo, Ana. *Peel My Love Like an Onion: A Novel.* New York: Random House, 1999.

Esquivel, Laura. *Like Water for Chocolate: A Novel in Monthly Installments, with Recipes, Romances, and Home Remedies.* Trans. Carol Christensen & Thomas Christensen. New York: Random House, 1992.

Friedensohn, Doris. "Chapulines, Mole, and Pozole: Mexican Cuisines and the Gringa Imagination." *Pilaf, Pozole, and Pad Thai: American Women and Ethnic Food.* Ed. Sherrie A. Inness. Amherst: U of Massachusetts P, 2001. 165–174.

Martínez, Demetria. *Mother Tongue.* New York: Ballantine Books, 1994.

Ortiz Cofer, Judith. *The Latin Deli: Prose and Poetry.* New York: W. W. Norton, 1993.

Santiago, Esmeralda. *Almost a Woman.* New York: Random House, 1998.

——. *When I Was Puerto Rican.* New York: Random House, 1993.

New Ways of Telling: Latinas' Narratives of Exile and Return

Jacqueline Stefanko

In the liminality of this moment in history, when discourses, disciplines, and politics converge and contend with one another, when border-crossing has become a site of resistant and liberatory possibilities, I see Latin American women writing in the United States mapping out paradigmatic shifts in the ways we read and write. The work of Julia Alvarez, Cristina Garcia, Rosario Morales, and Aurora Levins Morales reveals the processes of migrant souls, weaving together the threads of memory, history, and narration at the crossroads of feminisms, postcolonialisms, and socialisms. At the same time, these authors' works highlight the intercultural questions of identity that emerge at these crossroads. Each of these women writers is a world traveler, having emigrated or been exiled from a Latin American country to the United States with the process of return an ever-present, physical and/or textual possibility.[1] These authors use their skills and experiences as world travelers to take us "to places of subjectivity that shift and hyphenate into the worlds of others."[2] As Edward Said reminds us, "exile, immigration and the crossing of boundaries are experiences that can . . . provide us with new narrative forms or, in John Berger's phrase, with other ways of telling."[3]

I propose to read Julia Alvarez's *In the Time of the Butterflies* and *How the Garcia Girls Lost Their Accents*, Cristina Garcia's *Dreaming in Cuban*, and Rosario Morales and Aurora Levins Morales's *Getting Home Alive* as new ways of telling. As hybrid selves who cross and recross borders of language and culture, these Latina writers create hybrid texts in order to "survive in diaspora," to use Donna Haraway's term, seeking to heal the fractures and ruptures resulting from exile and dispersal.[4] Polyphonic narration, permeable borders (between genres, among national identifications, in the dialectic of self and other), and negotiation of the gestures of what James Clifford calls "traveling/dwelling" are the attributes that distinguish these texts as new ways of telling.[5] Migration becomes the means by which memories are narrated in specific historical contexts, infusing the empty/open/silent spaces in history, discourses, and politics with resistant and alternative paradigms.

As migrant souls traveling/dwelling in diverse cultural spaces, Latina writers become embedded within the process of translation, the linguistic border-crossing that necessarily accompanies any other shifts across boundaries. If we consider translation to be an alteration in signification, an act of decentering one's self and playing with language, then to translate may be the Derridean "affirmation of the play of the world and of the innocence of becoming, the affirmation of a world of signs without fault, without truth, and without origin which is offered to an active interpretation."[6] Translation enables the author to perceive the occluded fiction of a stable center, the fictive purity of self-presence, while simultaneously enabling her to enter into dialogues with the multiple aspects of self revealed through displacement. As Latinas and feminists, the authors realize, as Haraway has observed, that "releasing the play of writing is deadly serious." Haraway explains that the "poetry and stories of U.S. women of color are repeatedly about writing, about access to the power to signify, but this time that power must be neither phallic nor innocent."[7] Morales and Levins Morales's suggestive title, *Getting Home Alive*, indicates an awareness and negotiation of the messiness of playing with language and of the power of writing as boundary-crossing where the terrain is impure, anomalous, unstable, and potentially hazardous.

Due to the shifting, unstable terrain they inhabit, Latin American (migrant) women writers question and reject the assumption that a unitary, synthesizing narrator is capable of telling the stories they have to disclose, instead opting for a narrative stance that includes multiple voicings. Their utilization of multiple narrators contributes to the critique that "the theory of the subject of consciousness as a unitary and synthesizing agent of knowledge is always already a posture of domination."[8] Polyphonic narration is one mode of crossing the threshold into the anomalous, impure, and unstable. That crossing enables the reader and writer to participate in the breaking down of constructed, pure boundaries and to engage in complex heterogeneous dialogues. Telling the story of three generations of Cuban women and their experiences with revolution and immigration in *Dreaming in Cuban*, Cristina Garcia utilizes a mixture of third person character-specific narrators, first person narrators, and epistolary interjections to convey the rich texture of subject positionalities and the multiple worlds where the subject of consciousness travels. Julia Alvarez explores throughout *How the Garcia Girls Lost Their Accents* the effects of heterotopicality upon four sisters traveling/dwelling between the Dominican Republic and the United States. Third person character-specific narrative pieces engage mobility as the novel progresses backward through time and experience in order to enable first person narrators to emerge and take over the telling of their memories. Similarly, *In the Time of the Butterflies*, Alvarez's second novel, is comprised of the first person voices of the four sisters known as Las Mariposas because of their political activism in the Dominican Republic. Yet, Dede, the sister who survives, speaks through a third-person character-specific narrator until the end of the text when, after her sisters' memories have been narrated, her own voice emerges to articulate "I" Explicitly autobiographical, *Getting Home Alive* is the cross-fertilization of two women's voices, Rosario's and Aurora's, mother and daughter respectively, speaking in several tongues and several genres. The polyphony of each of these texts elucidates the subject of consciousness as a weave of multiple sites of identification and contestation.

Underlying the construction of each of these polyphonic narratives there appears to be what Clifford describes as "unresolved historical dialogues between continuity and disruption, essence and positionality, homogeneity and differences (cross-cutting 'us' and 'them') [that] characterize diasporic articulations."[9] Due to the processes of exile and migration, which establish the ambivalent gesture of traveling/dwelling, Alvarez, Garcia, Morales, and Levins Morales write in diaspora, and their texts are expressions of the dialogues generated by their negotiation of such traveling. In an essay on the black women writer's literary tradition, Mae Gwendolyn Henderson explains that "what is at once characteristic and suggestive about black women's writing is its interlocutory, or dialogic character, reflecting not only a relationship with the 'other(s),' but an internal dialogue with the plural aspects of self that constitute the matrix of black female subjectivity."[10] While she is speaking specifically about African American women authors, her insights appear to be quite relevant to the literature being produced by Latinas involved in cultures of displacement, transplantation, and return. The creation of multiple narrators can be considered an integral part of the authors' performance of both their external and internal diasporic dialogues, suggesting that utilizing the multiple voices is a manifestation of the subject of consciousness-shifting among multiple positions. Furthermore, as readers and critics, we must become diasporic in our apprehension and comprehension of their texts and accept Carol Boyce Davies's assertion that African American and Caribbean women's writing "should be read as a series of boundary crossings and not as a fixed geographical, ethnically or nationally bound category of writing.[11] Both the dialogic, diasporic narrative created by the author and the dialogic, diasporic self expressed via the text can be claimed as hybrids.

Mestizaje, the concept of hybridity culturally specific for Latinas, involves the conception of a "multiple subject who is not fragmented."[12] The cover picture and opening narrative piece of *Getting Home Alive* provide insight into the terrain of mestizaje as a site where the discourses and politics of feminisms, postcolonialisms, and socialisms converge in their affiliation and modification of one another and diverge in their contestation and resistance to one another. The cover picture of the quilt introduces us to the recurrent imagery of sewing/ weaving as a metaphor for both hybridity and narrative. The activity of sewing/weaving is gender specific with class connotations, implying a space of intersection between feminism and socialism. Like the mestiza identity presented in-process autobiographically by the Puerto Rican–Jewish American Morales and Levins Morales, the strengths of the quilt are its lack of homogeneity and the fact that the pieces that compose it cannot be separated from one another without losing their integrity. Furthermore, the image of the quilt illustrates the creative process that stitches diverse elements of different shapes, colors, and textures together to produce a distinct and meaningful whole that is more than the sum of its parts. The process evoked with this image informs our understanding of hybrid selves and hybrid narratives, as it does the hybridization of discourses and politics. As Lourdes Rojas points out, the verb in Spanish for "to knit" is *tejer*, from the Latin *texere*, which has the same root as *texto*, the Spanish word for text.[13] As major contributors to the polyphonic character of hybrid selves and hybrid narratives, interreference and interlinguistic play emerge as important facets of Morales and Levins Morales's writing as traveler/dwellers at the crossroads of feminisms, postcolonialisms, and socialisms. As readers and critics, we must participate in interlinguistic play if we are to apprehend and comprehend their subtle and complex displacements and infusions of discursive meaning.

"Wolf," the opening narrative piece of *Getting Home Alive*, written by Aurora Levins Morales, picks up a parallel thread in the discussion of hybridity. Levins Morales ends "Wolf" and begins the rest of the text with the emphatic statement, "I must make them see the wolf's nature. I must tell them this story" (*GHA*, 16). By placing this statement at the end of the opening narrative piece and at the beginning of the rest of the text, Levins Morales allows the wolf, represented as a shape-shifter, to tell the story of multiple transformations as a mode of survival and of resistance. As an emblem for her "true self," the wolf's story is also her own (*GHA*, 16). Facing the forces of extinction, encountering racism, sexism, colonization, and elitism, Levins Morales has acquired the necessary skill of shifting shapes or, in other words connotative of diaspora, she has learned to be a world-traveler in order to survive. By extension, the entire autobiographical text is her story of self, the one she must tell in order to survive. By expanding the story she must tell to include the entire text, Levins Morales calls attention to the text as a shape-shifter as well. We must attune ourselves to the negotiation of her writing's boundary-crossings and metamorphoses. By evoking the oral tradition of storytelling as an endangered species, akin to the wolf in this piece, Levins Morales realizes Rojas's statement that "oral stories are no longer viable testimonies of these women's experiences, for they can no longer endure to bear witness to a reality defined by the constant struggle to survive at the crossroads."[14] Instead, she commits herself to preservation through the written word, narrating the creative and liberatory power of what is multiple, anomalous, and hybrid.

While the viability of oral tradition for the transmission of women's stories can be questioned in these turbulent times, we can acknowledge that patriarchal, colonial, and neocolonial recorded stories have also failed to testify and/or represent women's memory. In praise of Julia Alvarez's *In the Time of the Butterflies*, Sandra Cisneros writes, "All Latinas are indebted to her for resisting the amnesia that has been our history." Although this statement critiques the masculinist, nationalist, and racist biases of historical records, which have resulted in the absence of women of color's voices and stories, the concept of amnesia also has other implications within the context of exile. In her postscript, Alvarez discusses her motivations in producing this novel. First, she identifies herself and her family as "exiles from the tyranny of Trujillo" (*ITB*, 323). Second, she connects her family's politics and their forced escape from the Dominican Republic to the four invented Mirabel sisters, their political activities, and their subsequent deaths four months after their escape. Then, her returns to the Dominican Republic become entwined with stories about the courage of Las Mariposas. Exile, translation, and migration mark profound changes in consciousness, as Benedict Anderson explains: "All profound changes in consciousness, by their very nature, bring with them characteristic amnesias. Out of such oblivions, in specific historical circumstances, spring narratives . . . Out of this estrangement [of continuity and memory loss] comes a conception of personhood, *identity* which, because it cannot be 'remembered,' must be narrated."[15] Alvarez seems especially conscious that in order to resist amnesia, one must narrate or reinvent both self and history: "For I wanted to immerse my readers in an epoch in the life of the Dominican Republic that I believe can only finally be understood by fiction, only finally be redeemed by the imagination" (*ITB*, 324). As I suggested earlier, the amnesia produced by the diasporic cultures of Latinas gets negotiated within the text through polyphony. Living at the crossroads, migrating between the United States and the Dominican Republic, establishes a dialogue between the author and the aspects of otherness within herself; between the Mirabel sisters; and between the author, the sisters, and the readers who are specifically English-speaking. The text becomes not only an example of writing as boundary-crossing, but also the vehicle by which the author crosses boundaries, negotiates the estrangement of continuity and memory loss, and traverses the subject of consciousness.

Alvarez's first novel, the loosely autobiographical *How the Garcia Girls Lost Their Accents*, engages in a similar dynamic between exile and return, narrating what cannot be remembered. Like the *Butterflies*, the four central characters are sisters. The text opens with "Antojos," the story of Yolanda's return to the island as an adult in 1989. Immediately we are placed at the crossroads of interreference and interlinguistic play. Several pages into the narrative piece we are given a discussion of the meaning of the word *antojo* that negotiates race, class, gender, and migration:

> "What's an *antojo*?" Yolanda asks.
> See! Her aunts are right. After so many years away, she is losing her Spanish . . .
> "An *antojo* is like a craving for something you have to eat . . ."
> An *antojo*, one of the older aunts continues, is a very old Spanish word "from before your United States was even thought of," she adds tartly. "In fact, in the countryside, you'll still find some *campesinos* using the word in the old sense. Altagracia! . . ."
> The maid obeys. "In my *campo* we say a person has an *antojo* when they are taken over by *un santo* who wants something." (*HGGLTA*, 8)

The conversation between the aunts, Yolanda, and the maid over the meaning of the word *antojo* enables the author to engage in a dialogue that both affirms and contests the multiple aspects of herself. Yolanda attempts to resolve the ambivalence inherent to such a dialogue by re-inventing the word to convey her desire for home.

Yolanda has returned to the Dominican Republic seeking to remedy her feelings of displacement, which she believes are the reason "she and her sisters have led such turbulent lives—so many husbands, homes, jobs, wrong turns among them" (*HGGLTA*, 11). Yet, the tone of nostalgia expressed in regard to finding an unspoiled home in the landscape of the Dominican countryside with its rural campesinos is countered by the author's attention to details of cross-cultural permeability and interaction: "In the glow of the headlights, Yolanda makes out the figure of the old woman in the black square of her doorway, waving good-bye. And above the picnic table on a near post, the Palmolive woman's skin gleams a rich white; her head is still thrown back, her mouth still opened as if she is calling someone over a great distance" (*HGGLTA*, 23). The contrast between distance and proximity, the incongruity of the old woman and the Palmolive woman, the difference in skin color, privilege, and commodification heightens our awareness of the imperialistic invasion of United States commercialism into the Dominican Republic after the island was liberated from Trujillo. Within this neocolonial-colonial context, the third person character-specific narrator destabilizes Yolanda's return to the island, allowing us to question the totalizing boundaries of what Benedict R. Anderson calls the "imagined community," as well as Yolanda's desire for origin.[16] She has, after all, lost her accent. On another level, the author may be decentering and questioning her own return to the island via a narrative that moves backward in time and place to the memories of the four sisters before they were forced to leave their home in the Dominican Republic. By purposefully fictionalizing her own historical, autobiographical life story in a polyphonic novel, Alvarez creates a new way of telling that crosses the boundaries between genres, between individual and community, between national identifications, and between continuity and disruption, giving definition to her writing as diasporic articulation. As English-speaking readers, we must be wary of our contributions to the narrative and be prepared to question our willing acceptance and participation in colonizing gestures that attempt to occlude the border-crossings that are occurring.

Cristina Garcia begins *Dreaming in Cuban* with Celia scanning the sea coast of Cuba for signs of U.S. invasion, giving prominence to the issue of borders and their permeability on the first page of her novel. The fishing boats Celia sees, "the Niña, the Pinta and the Santa María," invoke the issue of colonization as they conjure the image of Columbus arriving (*DIC*, 4). The historical events of colonization, revolution, and threatened invasion entwine around the personal issue of family separation and exile. Celia's commitment to protecting her country's boundaries becomes ambivalent with the realization of the costs of exile: "Frustrated El Líder went home, rested his pitching arm, and started a revolution in the mountains. Because of this, Celia thinks, her husband will be buried in stiff, foreign earth. Because of this, their children and their grandchildren are nomads" (*DIC*, 6–7). While "nomads" connotes mobility, there is also the indication of a lack of connection, of home. Celia thinks specifically of her granddaughter Pilar and of the losses of acculturation that accompany immigration. Yet, despite the seemingly inflexible boundaries separating Celia in communist Cuba and Pilar in capitalist New York, there exists a bond between grandmother and granddaughter that remains tenuously elastic and fluid: "She knows that Pilar keeps a diary in the lining of her

winter coat, hidden from her mother's scouring eyes. In it, Pilar records everything. This pleases Celia. She closes her eyes and speaks to her granddaughter, imagines her words as slivers of light piercing the murky night" (*DIC*, 7).
Significantly, the telepathic thread connecting Celia to Pilar is conceived as
textuality and creativity.

Pilar, speaking in the first person, reinforces our awareness of the connection between her and Celia. Narrating a memory of herself as a baby with nan-
nies in Cuba, she says, "They called me *brujita*, little witch. I stared at them,
tried to make them go away. I remember thinking, Okay, I'll start with their
hair, make it fall out strand by strand. They always left wearing kerchiefs to
cover their bald patches" (*DIC*, 28). *La bruja* is a powerful figure within Latino
cultures who is often hated and feared because of her creative abilities to conjure and conceive by playing with language. If we identify Celia and Pilar as
brujas, then we realize that Celia fears acculturation because of the losses of
language, traditions, and knowledges, which are neither phallic nor innocent,
that are the fund of the bruja's powers to conjure with alternative paradigms
and activate change with active interpretations of language. Yet, Pilar demonstrates her memory as a bruja when she critiques the biases of history and
suggests she knows other(s') stories that have been silenced: "If it were up to
me, I'd record other things. Like the time there was a freak hailstorm in the
Congo and the women took it as a sign that they should rule. Or the life stories of prostitutes in Bombay" (*DIC*, 28). This knowledge appears to be part
of Pilar's inheritance from her grandmother, an inheritance that has significant implications for narrating memory, resisting amnesia, and constructing
polyphonic texts. As brujas, Celia and Pilar share knowledges that have the
power to imagine community in alternative, transnational ways, thus perme-
ating boundaries and allowing us to question the construction of borders as
pure and inflexible.

In two separate but related poems, Aurora Levins Morales and Rosario
Morales speak directly to issues of borders and identification. In the confrontational "I Am What I Am," Rosario defiantly asserts her acceptance of all
the pieces of herself without the need for external approval: "I am what I am
and you can't take it away with all the words and sneers at your command"
(*GHA*, 138). She rejects society's fragmentation of her into pure parts, seeing this as an exercise in domination. Yet, she has had to struggle in order to
achieve this straddling stance and precarious balance: "I am what I am and
I am U.S. American I haven't wanted to say it because if I did you'd take away
the Puerto Rican" (*GHA*, 138). Never having believed in or experienced as her
reality the inflexible, unquestionable boundaries of "separation as purity," to
use Lugones's phrase, has enabled Rosario to make the conceptual leap out of
dichotomous patterns of thinking.[17] Forcing the reader to rethink the meaning
of several "national" identifications in her terms, she helps us to move out of
the binary mode of classification toward hybrid, both/and conceptualizations
as well. Puerto Rican identity is a piece in the mosaic of herself that has been
altered, made new by her experiences: "I am Boricua as Boricuas come from
the isle of Manhattan and I croon sentimental tangos in my sleep and Afro-
Cuban beats in my blood" (*GHA*, 138). The multiplicity of her identifications

establishes Morales on the hyphen, shifting among the many worlds that she inhabits and altering them in the process. The text she creates to express her hybrid identity and its creative alterations is the instrument of her agency in healing the fractures and splits caused by diasporic dispersal within the context of U.S. imperialism, racism, sexism, and elitism.

Similarly, Aurora Levins Morales expresses a hybridity of self in "Child of the Americas." She identifies herself as a "light-skinned mestiza of the Caribbean, / a child of many diaspora, born into this continent at a crossroads" (*GHA*, 50). While diaspora connotes displacement, crossroads connote confluence. Together, these two gestures situate Aurora as a traveler/dweller within a specific historical context. Although she claims her history—African, Taina, European—and acknowledges that her history has shaped her, she also asserts that she is something new, as Gloria Anzaldúa described it, as "something more than mere duality or a synthesis of duality."[18] Levins Morales expands our ethnocentric definition of America by stressing the multiplicity and heterotopicality of the spaces she travels/dwells in: "I am a U.S. Puerto Rican Jew, / a product of the ghettos of New York I have never known. / . . . I am of Latinoamerica, rooted in the history of my continent: / I speak from that body" (*GHA*, 50). Like her mother, Levins Morales has engaged textuality in order to express her hybridity and testify to the imaginative ambiguity of the mestiza subject of consciousness.

Both Morales and Levins Morales convey the power of performing mestizaje through polyphonic speaking and writing. Morales speaks from the crossroads of "yiddish, and spanish and fine refined college educated english and irish," finding poetic inspiration and an empowering strength in the confluence (*GHA*, 138). Levins Morales's poetic voice gains similar sustenance from her bilingualism: "I speak English with passion: it's the tongue of my consciousness, / a flashing knife blade of crystal, my tool, my craft. / . . . Spanish is in my flesh, / ripples from my tongue, lodges in my hips: / the language of garlic and mangoes, / the singing in my poetry" (*GHA*, 50). Each strain contributes something distinctive to her voice, and she refuses to deny either influence. Furthermore, she asserts the hybridity of her voice, the inseparability of her bilingualism: "My first language was spanglish" (*GHA*, 50). For both Morales and Levins Morales, heterogeneity, interpenetration, and the creative power of imagining borders as porous facilitate new ways of telling self and constructing community. The subject of consciousness, which emerges from the rich and complex texture of their work, is not unitary and synthesizing, but is rather mobile, or in Kathy Ferguson's words, "temporal, moving across and along axes of power (which are themselves in motion) without fully residing in them . . . relational, produced through shifting yet enduring encounters and connections, never fully captured by them . . . ambiguous: messy and multiple, unstable but perservering."[19] As Morales and Levins Morales attempt to "get home alive," they engage mobility when difference denies any easy, stable resting place of identification.

Yolanda, the first sister to engage in first person narration in Alvarez's *How the Garcia Girls Lost Their Accents*, also demonstrates the mobility of the subject of consciousness. The transition from third person, character-specific narration to first person voice occurs after the narrative piece in which Yolanda is shown negotiating issues of language, specifically the border-crossing of translation and bilingualism. Within this context, the issue of naming as a process of identity starts the piece: "Yolanda, nicknamed *Yo* in Spanish, misunderstood *Joe* in English, doubled and pronounced like the toy, *Yoyo*—or when forced to select from a rack of personalized key chains, *Joey*" (*HGGLTA*, 68). As Yolanda's names proliferate on the page, we begin to see the multiplicity of her identity. We must also reckon with the ethnocentric irony of "personalized" when one is Latino and not Anglo. And as the passage continues, we realize the struggle Yolanda must engage in to not be fragmented in a society that marginalizes her. Involved in a dialogue with her Anglo-American lover, Yolanda is forced into an act of translation in order to place herself:

> "Sky, I want to be the sky."
> "That's not allowed . . . Your own rules: you've got to rhyme with your name."
> "I"—she pointed to herself—"rhymes with the sky!"
> "But not with Joe!" . . .
> "*Yo* rhymes with *cielo* in Spanish." Yo's words fell into the dark, mute cavern of John's mouth. *Cielo, cielo,* the word echoed. And Yo was running, like the mad, into the safety of her first tongue, where the proudly monolingual John could not catch her, even if he tried. (*HGGLTA*, 72)

The bilingualism of Yolanda's chosen name rhyme and her migration into her (m)other tongue demonstrate her abilities as a border-crosser. Implicitly, the author appears to be asking us to critique the practices of domination that maintain the arrogant and fictional purity of monolingualism as the respectable norm via the censure of the ambiguity and creativity of bilingualism as madness.

Yolanda's transversal of language results in John's condemnation of her as crazy. Their difference and his power as a white Anglo-American male threatens to split Yolanda. As the narrative piece ends, Yolanda and John are in the process of separating, and Yolanda gives us an expression of the pain of fragmentation: "When she left her husband, Yo wrote a note, *I'm going to my folks till my head-slash-heart clear. She revised the note: I'm needing some space, some time, until my head-slash-heart-slash-soul*—No, no, no, she didn't want to divide herself anymore, three persons in one Yo" (*HGGLTA*, 78). Significantly, *Yo* is the Spanish word for the first person pronoun "I." Interjecting this odd epistolary first person discourse within a third person narrative piece, the author appears to be signaling the performance of curdling, where the subject of consciousness asserts the many in the indivisible. Lugones theorizes curdling to be an impure separation, one that has the resistant and liberatory power to assert the multiple and reject fragmentation into pure parts.[20] Presenting Yolanda as a curdled being, as an example of mestizaje, the author suggests a continuum relationship between "she," the third person, and "I," the first person, where subject positions are not split-separated. Within this presentation of the alteration of the self/other dialectic, Lugones says "there is the distance of metacomment, autoreflection, looking at oneself in someone else's mirror and back in one's own, of self-aware experimentation.[21] Through the creative medium of language, the active interpretation of translation, Yolanda is established on the hyphen where she can shift among subject positions and worlds. Consequently, she gains the self-reflexivity necessary to emerge fully as a first person narrator and enter into dialogues with the multiple aspects of her Yo.

As a diasporic interlocutor, Yolanda is located in the midst of the interaction and contradiction between the autoreflection of homogeneity and difference. Coming to feminist consciousness during her teenage years in the United States, Yolanda, along with her sisters, negotiates the specific Latino cultural paradigms of patriarchy and the specific American strains of racism. Class combines with gender and ethnicity so that when Fifi, the youngest sister, is sent to live on the island, the three older sisters fear "that Fifi was caving in to family pressure and regressing into some nice third world girl" (*HGGLTA*, 118). They see Fifi losing her streak of independence, her strong-willed rebelliousness, which they associate with their "American" identities, in contrast to the island's prescribed gender roles, which they assume conform to the marianismo/machismo dialectic. Carla, Sandi, and Yolanda forge a feminist bond of solidarity to battle machismo and the patriarchal indoctrination of their sister. Conceptualizing their actions as a revolution, they liberate Sofia from the allure and seeming safety of class-defined traditions: "We look at each other as if to say, 'She'll get over it.' Meaning Manuel, meaning her fury at us, meaning her fear of her own life. Like ours, it lies ahead of her like a wilderness just before the first explorer sets foot on the virgin sand" (*HGGLTA*, 132). In this narrative piece, we can see unresolved historical dialogues at work. As first world feminists, the sisters refuse to allow Sofia to submit to the self-abnegation of docility. They demand that she act as a full subject, with the power to determine her own desires. Yet, the metaphor of life as a female landscape to be penetrated by the "exploring" first-world feminist explicitly invokes the history of Conquistadors and imperialism. The girls' return to the island is destabilized and their feminist practices become problematically associated with the gestures of colonization. The homogeneous, essential "nice third world girl" is placed in juxtaposition to the positionality of the liberated first world feminist, and difference is used to split "us" and "them." By making her metaphor so conspicuous, the author compels us to question our involvement in accepting the assumption that first world women are more liberated than third world women, that is, to question our own investment and participation in the processes of colonization.

Offering her readers textual instruction in what Lugones calls "loving perception" (as opposed to "arrogant perception" and its colonizing force), Alvarez details the development of feminist-socialist consciousnesses and practices in four sisters in the Dominican Republic in her second novel, *In the Time of the Butterflies*.[22] As Alvarez writes in her postscript: "I would hope that through this fictionalized story I will bring acquaintance of these famous sisters to English-speaking readers. November 25th, the day of their murder, is observed in many Latin American countries as the International Day Against Violence Towards Women. Obviously, these sisters, who fought one tyrant, have served as models for women fighting against injustices of all kinds" (*ITB*, 324). Patria, Minerva, Mate, and Dede come alive in first person narrative pieces to resist amnesia and colonization. The author explicitly constructs their narrative in order to present her English-speaking audience with an alternative paradigm of feminist-socialism informed by postcolonial discourse, which may act as a bridge connecting women without denying differences.

Dede begins the novel in third person, character-specific narration, awaiting the arrival of a *gringa dominicana* who wants to question her about her sisters. If Alvarez is representing herself through this hybrid designation, she distances herself by several layers from the telling, perhaps to avoid the gestures of colonization that say, "they cannot represent themselves so they must be represented." Furthermore, as the hybrid gringa dominicana, she blurs the boundaries between "us" and "them" in the performance of her own subject status and locates herself, as Ferguson explains, "in relation to the moving trajectories of power and resistance via circumstances of proximity and distance, restlessness and rootedness, separation and connection."[23] As we shall see, each of the sisters are mobile subjects as well.

Dede's narrator, anticipating the questions of the gringa dominicana, utilizes the collective ghost voices of past interviewers to articulate a central question of the novel: "Usually they leave, satisfied, without asking the prickly questions that have left Dede lost in her memories for weeks at a time, searching for the answer. Why, they inevitably ask in one form or another, why are you the one who survived?" (*ITB*, 5). The answer lies in the negotiation of personal and collective history because by surviving, Dede enables memory, the narration of the stories of Las Mariposas. Remembering is explicitly characterized as narration as Dede constructs her sisters as if they are characters in a play and describes memory as a movie she can watch in her mind's eye. Continuing the metaphor, the woman interviewer asks Dede to recount a mininarrative, and Dede rewinds her memory like a video tape to time "zero" (*ITB*, 7). Ground zero is characterized as a moment "before the future began," and we are placed in the site of estrangement between continuity and memory loss (*ITB*, 8). As the scene ends, "A chill goes through her, for she feels it in her bones, the future is now beginning. By the time it is over, it will be the past, and she doesn't want to be the only one left to tell their story" (*ITB*, 10). The prophetic tone and the confusion of time signals a shift, as if the actors are about to come onto the stage.

Minerva's voice is the first to emerge from oblivion, and her opening paragraphs set the tone for the feminist-socialist consciousness of the Mirabel sisters. The girls' privilege of being allowed, by their father, access to education is envisioned as a blessing in a religious metaphor that invokes the enmeshed patriarchal institutions of the family and the church. Minerva details the restrictions placed upon girls and expresses desire for autonomy, freedom, and self-determination. Unlike the rabbit she attempts to force into freedom, she refuses to become accustomed to the confines of prescribed gender roles. A specific kind of education becomes the site of emancipation: "And that's how I got free. I don't mean just going to sleepaway school on a train with a trunkful of new things. I mean in my head after I got to Inmaculada and met Sinita and saw what happened to Lina and realized that I'd just left a small cage to go into a bigger one, the size of our whole country" (*ITB*, 13). Thus, the patriarchal confines of the family and the church are placed in direct connection to the patriarchal and totalitarian functioning of the state, establishing a relationship between feminism and socialism.

The knowledge Minerva gains while at school is the result of her relationship with two women. Realizing the occlusions and obfuscations of history will deny her/story, Sinita tells Minerva the secret of Trujillo—his violent rise to power, his practices of terrorism and tyranny over those who oppose him—and narrates her personal memories of murder. Utilizing the oral tradition of testimonial to fill in the silence of history, Sinita provides Minerva instruction in the alternative paradigms of feminist-socialism. After hearing Sinita's story, Minerva says, "sure enough, my complications had started" (*ITB*, 20). While "complications" is clearly a euphemism for female menstruation, the coincidence of Minerva's physical awareness and political awareness invokes the complications of knowledge and power within the context of Trujillo's repressive regime. Minerva, as a mobile subject of consciousness, will negotiate the moving trajectories of power and resistance throughout the novel.

Lina's story continues Minerva's education about Trujillo. The beautiful, physically mature and adored Lina is spotted by Trujillo and chosen by him to become one of his many mistresses. Used and abandoned, Lina ends up locked away in a mansion behind high iron gates, designated *pobrecita* by her friends (*ITB*, 23). Lina's story reinforces the enmeshing of sexuality with issues of knowledge, power, and politics, thus securing a foundation for Minerva's feminist-socialism. She attempts to protect herself from the possibility of sexual exploitation by hiding the development of her breasts so that "what happened to Lina Lovatón would never happen" to her (*ITB*, 23). She also begins to engage in a critique of the government and the record of history that seeks to deny her memories of herstory. This critique quickly leads to her involvement in politically subversive activities.

Maria Teresa, or Mate, as she is known throughout most of the text, is the second sister to speak in first person. Her narrative pieces are presented as journal entries in a series of diaries given to her by Minerva. Alvarez intensifies the power of her polyphonic novel by utilizing multiple narrators as well as multiple narrative forms. The diary form enables her to heighten the sense of autoreflection. Aptly, the initial diary is a present for Mate's first communion, and she writes: "Minerva says keeping a diary is also a way to reflect and reflection deepens one's soul. It sounds so serious. I suppose now that I've got one I'm responsible for, I have to expect some changes" (*ITB*, 30). Within the context of the church, we are once again made aware of subtle subversions of patriarchy, for the deepening of the soul toward which Mate is religiously instructed is quite different than the consciousness she attains. While Mate's narrated memories seem superficial at first, the evolution of her political awareness becomes evident via the process of writing. Gaining knowledge of sexuality and political power, Mate loses her naïveté along with her first diary and writes: "Minerva was right. My soul has gotten deeper since I started writing in you. But this is what I want to know that not even Minerva knows.

What do I do now to fill up that hole?" (*ITB*, 43). Political activism and the collective struggle against tyranny, although motivated by romance for Mate, seem to supply the sustenance she seeks.

Patria, the third Mariposa to emerge in telling, is guided by a passion for God and an altruistic faith, as well as by the different passion of sexual desire. The teachings of the church direct Patria toward the appropriate spheres of marriage and religious service. Her patriarchal indoctrination causes her, at first, to accept the belief that women should not be involved in the public affairs of politics. Yet, after she miscarries, Patria suffers a crisis in faith and her feminist-socialist consciousness begins to grow:

> That moment, I understood [Minerva's] hatred. My family had not been personally hurt by Trujillo, just as before losing my baby, Jesus had not taken anything away from me. But others had been suffering great losses. There were the Perozos, not a man left in that family. And Martínez Reyna and his wife murdered in their bed, and thousands of Haitians massacred at the border, making the river, they say, still run red—¡*Ay Dios santo!* I had heard, but I had not believed . . . How could our loving, all-powerful Father allow us to suffer so? I looked up, challenging Him. And the two faces [of the Good Shepherd and El Jefe] had merged! (*ITB*, 53)

While on a pilgrimage to Virgencita, Patria asks for guidance and a sign that will renew her faith. Looking back at the "hundreds of weary, upturned faces" who have packed the church to pray, Patria finds resolution to her spiritual crisis as she reorients her faith toward the masses and realizes that the people's liberty is sacred, worthy of devotion and imbued with the divine. Thus, a third sister's political consciousness is born of subversions of patriarchy.

Although Dede similarly experiences the growth of consciousness, she chooses to remain loyal to tradition, standing by her husband and his decision to remain disengaged from the political sedition. When Minerva, Mate, their husbands, and Patria's husband are imprisoned and tortured, Dede realizes that "whether she joined their underground or not, her fate was bound up with the fates of her sisters" (*ITB*, 193). She also acknowledges that her fate will be different and that "if they died, she would not want to go on living without them," but would have to (Alvarez 193). After the release of Minerva and Mate, and the subsequent murder of Minerva, Mate, and Patria as they return from visiting their husbands in prison, Dede questions her choices, believing she lacked the courage to join her sisters in their struggle. Yet, at the end of the novel, Dede recognizes courage as her responsibility to narrate and renew the story of Las Mariposas. The story she enables embodies the feminist-socialist paradigms her sisters generated in their politically subversive activities, thus establishing the resistant and liberatory power of narrative. Coming full circle to the future prophesied at the beginning, Dede looks around her for evidence of the revolution her sisters fought and died for. Seeing only reform, neocolonialism, and the losses of her country's collective memory, Dede asks, "was it for this, the sacrifice of the butterflies?" (*ITB*, 318). As English-speaking readers, as first-world feminists, we must examine our responsibility in failing to connect with the rest of the hemisphere in the coalitional politics that could provide the means for more effective change. Yet, I believe, as Alvarez appears to, that the sacrifice of the butterflies has affected some real and important changes in the world and, at the very least, has resulted in this novel's resistance to amnesia.

For the characters of Garcia's *Dreaming in Cuban*, the costs and failings of revolution are equally important for acknowledging the power of narration. Exiled from Cuba as a small child, Pilar finds herself feeling connected to other exiles, the Jews who surround her in Brooklyn. As Amy Kaminsky theorizes in *Reading the Body Politic*, "language tells us that exile is its own location: people living out of their homeland are 'in exile' . . . the place of exile is defined by what is missing, not by what it contains."[24] As a condition of her displacement, Pilar does not feel at home in New York because she experiences this sense of absence in the missing presence of her grandmother Celia. Separated from Cuba and her grandmother by the "politicians and the generals who force events on us that structure our lives, that dictate the memories we'll have when we're old," Pilar's telepathic connection with Celia grows silent, and she is forced to engage in a quest to resolve her displacement (*DIC*, 138). As the first step in her journey, Pilar conceptualizes a special, almost tropical, light favored by her for painting as a "matrix light, a recombinant light that disintegrates hard lines and planes, rearranging objects to their essences" (*DIC*, 178). This conceptualization appears to participate in the unresolved historical dialogues characteristic of diasporic articulations as it negotiates between the impurity and fluidity of borders and the stability of essences. Pilar finds herself guided by this light to a botanica where she reconnects with her Afro-Cuban heritage and her patron spirit, Chango, the god of fire and lightening. Guided by Chango, Pilar begins to recuperate her telepathic powers: "I can hear fragments of people's thoughts, glimpse scraps of the future . . . erratic as lightening" (*DIC*, 216). No longer a spiritual exile, she has the power to cross the boundaries separating her from Cuba and her grandmother. Without any explanation of the logistics of traveling to Cuba, Pilar and her mother arrive as if by magic and ritually bathe Celia, thus healing the rupture in communication: "I pull the covers over Abuela's shoulders, searching her face for a hint of my own . . . I know what my grandmother dreams. Of massacres in distant countries, pregnant women dismembered in the squares. Abuela Celia walks among them mute and invisible. The thatched roofs steam in the morning air" (*DIC*, 218). In Pilar's narration of Celia's dreams, we are not allowed to forget the harshest conditions, what Clifford describes as the "strong cultural, political and economic compulsions" that force people to travel and emerge as diasporic cultures.[25] We can also begin to see the creative discursive transformations emerging from the enmeshing of feminism, socialism, and postcolonial discourse as an implicit counterinsurgent force.

The violations and ruptures of exile entwine with the regenerative powers of the bruja, creating the complex weave of the text. Ending *Dreaming in Cuban* with a final epistolary interjection dated January 11, 1959, Celia writes to her long lost lover Gustavo, "The revolution is eleven days old. My grand-daughter, Pilar Puente del Pino, was born today. It is also my birthday. I am fifty years old. I will no longer write to you, mi amor. She will remember everything" (*DIC*, 245). Such an ending emphasizes cyclicality as opposed to closure. At the age of fifty, Celia passes the torch of "knowledge like the first fire" to her granddaughter (*DIC*, 222). She knows Pilar will be the next bruja, the next storyteller who will continue the narration of memory by filling in the silences and constructing alternative paradigms capable of generating resistant and liberatory possibilities. Celia's last gift to Pilar is a "box of letters she wrote to her onetime lover in Spain, but never sent" and "a book of poems she's had since 1930, when she heard Garcia Lorca read" (*ITB*, 235). The textuality of Pilar's entire inheritance from Celia implicitly enables her to construct the polyphonic narrative of the novel, continuing the cycle. Together the implicit author status of the character Pilar and the loose autobiographical threads that connect her to the author Garcia suggest that narrative is the vehicle by which the ruptures of exile can be healed and that the gesture of traveling/dwelling can be negotiated via the text.

Similarly, Alvarez ends *How the Garcia Girls Lost Their Accents* with Yolanda's voice emerging as implicit author, telescoping time and events into a thread of exile and return, traveling/dwelling. She writes: "At that hour and in that loneliness, I hear her, a black furred thing lurking in the corners of my life, her magenta mouth opening, wailing over some violation that lies at the center of my art" (*HGGLTA*, 290). The reference to the kitten conjures the image of Yolanda as a child ripping a kitten from its mother, just as she was ripped from her mother-land, mother-tongue. If we see, as Kaminsky does, in the writing of exile "a discourse of desire, a desire to recuperate, repair and return," then we must also accept the violation, the rupture, the dispersal, and negotiate each gesture of traveling/dwelling in narrative simultaneously.[26]

The works of Julia Alvarez, Cristina Garcia, Rosario Morales, and Aurora Levins Morales highlight the intercultural questions of identity that evolve from being "in-between," from the condition of hybridity. Needing to survive at the crossroads, "where one never belongs totally to one place, yet where one is able to feel an integral part of many places," they construct hybrid narratives capable of engaging the mobility of their subject of consciousness, textually negotiating the spiral of exile and return.[27] The process of autobiographical writing becomes the site and tongue of Levins Morales and Morales's struggle to get home alive, to be immigrants and inventors of countries, to enunciate *jibaro*, "meaning one who runs away to be free" (*GHA*, 54). Their coauthored narrative demonstrates the resistant and liberatory power of the mestiza subject of consciousness, utilizing the tools of feminism, socialism, and postcolonial discourse, and speaks from within their hybridization. When Pilar returns to Cuba in *Dreaming in Cuban* and for the first time dreams in Spanish, she realizes that Cuba, although it cannot be her home, will always be a part of her consciousness. She perceives Cuba and her cultural memory to be a place she can continually renew and re-invent through narrative, with her imagination. The spirits of the Mitabel sisters in Alvarez's *In the Time of the Butterflies* can finally come to rest long after their deaths because Dede, the sister who survived, acts as a medium through which their voices transcend death and oblivion to enact narrative. Each of these texts attempts to facilitate a return and a recovery from exile, not by recuperating an essential origin, although nostalgia is tempting, but by inventing through an active and imaginative interpretation a narrative of home, history, and memory. As new ways of telling that both displace and converge multiple voices, multiple genres, and multiple gestures, these texts by Latinas writing in the United States offer exciting opportunities for the continued development of the fertile interlocking of discourses, disciplines, and politics.

NOTES

1. I use the term "world traveler" in the sense used by Maria C. Lugones in "Playfulness, 'World-traveling,' and Loving Perception," in *Making Face, Making Soul/Haciendo Caras: Creative and Critical Perspectives by Feminists of Color*, ed. Gloria Anzaldúa (San Francisco: Aunt Lute Books, 1990), 390.

2. Christine Sylvester, "African and Western Feminisms: World-Traveling the Tendencies and Possibilities," *Signs* 20:4 (1995): 946.

3. Edward Said, "Representing the Colonized: Anthropology's Interlocutors," *Critical Inquiry* 15 (1989): 225.

4. Julia Alvarez, *In the Time of the Butterflies* (Chapel Hill: Algonquin Books, 1994), and *How the Garcia Girls Lost Their Accents* (New York: Plume, 1994); Cristina Garcia, *Dreaming in Cuban* (New York: Ballantine Books, 1992); and Rosario Morales and Aurora Levins Morales, *Getting Home Alive* (Ithica: Firebrand Books, 1986). Hereafter, all references to these works will be cited parenthetically in the text. Donna Haraway, "A Manifesto for Cyborgs: Science, Technology, and Socialist Feminism in the 1980's," in *Feminism/Postmodernism*, ed. Linda J. Nicholson (New York: Routledge, 1990), 212.

5. James Clifford, "Traveling Cultures," in *Cultural Studies*, ed. Lawrence Grossberg, Cary Nelson, and Paula A. Treichler (New York: Routledge, 1992), 108.

6. Jacques Derrida, "Structure, Sign and Play in the Discourse of the Human Sciences," in *Writing and Difference* (Chicago: University of Chicago Press, 1978), 121.

7. Haraway, "A Manifesto for Cyborgs," 217.

8. Norma Alarcón, "The Theoretical Subject(s) of *This Bridge Called My Back* and Anglo-American Feminism," in Anzaldúa, *Making Face, Making Soul*, 364.

9. Clifford, "Traveling Cultures," 108.

10. Mae Gwendolyn Henderson, "Speaking in Tongues: Dialogics Dialectics, and the Black Woman Writer's Literary Tradition," in *Feminists Theorize the Political*, ed. Judith Butler and Joan W. Scott (New York: Routledge, 1992), 145.

11. Carol Boyce Davies, *Black Women, Writing, and Identity: Migrations of the Subject* (New York: Routledge, 1994), 4.

12. Maria C. Lugones, "Purity, Impurity, and Separation," *Signs* 19:2 (1995): 473.

13. Lourdes Rojas, "Latinas at the Crossroads," in *Breaking Boundaries*, ed. Asunción Horno-Delgado (Amherst: University of Massachusetts Press, 1989), 171.

14. Rojas, "Latinas at the Crossroads," 166.

15. Benedict R. Anderson, *Imagined Communities: Reflections on the Origin and Spread of Nationalism* (New York: Verso, 1983), 204.

16. Anderson, *Imagined Communities*, 6.

17. Lugones, "Purity, Impurity, and Separation," 462.

18. Gloria Anzaldúa, *Borderlands/La Frontera: The New Mestiza* (San Francisco: Aunt Lute Books, 1987), 46.

19. Kathy E. Ferguson, *The Man Question: Visions of Subjectivity in Feminist Theory* (Berkeley: University of California Press, 1993), 154.

20. Lugones, "Purity, Impurity, and Separation," 460.

21. Lugones, "Purity, Impurity, and Separation," 478.

22. Lugones, "Playfulness, 'World-Traveling,' and Loving Perception," 391.

23. Ferguson, *The Man Question*, 161.

24. Amy Kaminsky, *Reading the Body Politic: Feminist Criticism and Latin American Women Writers* (Minneapolis: University of Minnesota Press, 1993), 30.

25. Clifford, "Traveling Cultures," 108.

26. Kaminsky, *Reading the Body Politic*, 33.

27. Rojas, "Latinas at the Crossroads," 172.

Gloria Anzaldúa's Queer Mestisaje

Ian Barnard

In the 1992 "queer issue" of *The Village Voice*, Dennis Cooper quotes Johnny Noxzema and Rex Boy characterizing the Canadian publication *BIMBOX*, which Noxzema and Rex Boy edited:

> You are entering a gay and lesbian-free zone. . . . Effective immediately, *BIMBOX* is at war against lesbians and gays. A war in which modern queer boys and queer girls are united against the prehistoric thinking and demented self-serving politics of the above-mentioned scum. *BIM-BOX* hereby renounces its past use of the term lesbian and/or gay in a positive manner. This is a civil war against the ultimate evil, and consequently we must identify us and them in no uncertain terms. . . . So, dear lesbian womon or gay man to whom perhaps *BIMBOX* has been inappropriately posted . . . prepare to pay dearly for the way you and your kind have fucked things up. (31)

Readers unfamiliar with recent debacles within lesbian and gay political circles might be forgiven for at first assuming this to be a particularly scurrilous instance of violent homophobia. But, of course, the *BIMBOX* editors are themselves gay, and anti-homophobic activists, and theirs is actually a fairly typical articulation of what has by now become a relatively familiar opposition in political and cultural realms between lesbian and gay activists and queer militants and, in academia, between lesbian and gay studies and queer theory.

The queer sensibility and aesthetic embodied in *BIMBOX* has been articulated and flaunted in the queer 'zines of the 1980s and 1990s—"alternative" lesbian, gay, bisexual, and transgender periodicals, often relatively cheaply produced and locally distributed, and usually espousing and embodying a militantly non-assimilationist ideology.[1] *BIMBOX* suggests its contempt for

---

"Gloria Anzaldúa's Queer *Mestisaje*" was first published in *MELUS: The Journal of the Society for the Study of the Multi-Ethnic Literature of the United States* and is reprinted here with the permission of *MELUS*.

the orthodox procedures of publication and distribution employed around much lesbian and gay writing that has attained corporate legitimacy by advertising itself as "free to those who deserve it" (qtd. in *Holy Titclamps Zine Explosion* 3). The titles alone of some of the other 'zines suggest their oppositional relationship not only to mainstream straight publishing and politics, but also to mainstream lesbian and gay publishing and politics: *Pansy Beat, Not Your Bitch, The nighttime, sniffling, sneezing, coughing, aching, stuffy-head, fever, so you can rest zine*. One of the lesbian 'zines calls itself *Up Our Butts*, a particularly rich title for readers who have followed the feminist sex wars between the journals *Off Our Backs* and *On Our Backs*, and the lawsuit between the two (see Brownworth)! To clarify its distance from the categories "lesbian" and "gay," the Minneapolis 'zine *Holy Titclamps* comes stamped with the instructions "file under 'queer,'" on its cover—presumably for the benefit of perplexed bookstore clerks! Destabilizations of lesbian and gay identity abound in the 'zines. *QT* promises an article on "the faggot who thought she was a lesbian." The contents of *Scab* #2 are described in a blurb for the 'zine as "Bitch Nation, anti-William Burroughs stuff, pro-gaybashing with map of gay areas, anti-SPEW convention article" (*Holy Titclamps* 9). [2]

The prevalence of sexism, racism, and classism in official lesbian and gay culture and politics, as much as in the hegemonic heterosexual establishment, is a frequent subject of the, 'zines. In the September/October 1992 issue of the 'zine *Infected Faggot Perspectives*, Christian Salvador, described as "a short, left-handed, 18 year old, Pilipino, cross-dressing, pimpleless whore who's been entertaining the idea of water-sports; part-time queer activist" writes:

> Early this last year I was introduced to west Hollywood—What is it?! It's two blocks of 21 and over white fags who don't even notice the existence of women standing two inches from them, much less little thing like me. . . . Well, West Hollywood don't look like where and how I'd like to celebrate my queerness. (8)

One of the most striking characteristics of the 'zines—and this is, perhaps, what sets them most apart from glossier, more mainstream lesbian and gay publications—is their difference from each other, their appeal to and identification with a very specialized readership *within* "the lesbian and gay community"—indeed, their contestation of the very idea that there is such an entity as a unified and unitary "lesbian and gay community," a totalization that has been repeatedly questioned for over a decade by white lesbians and queer people of color of all genders. The 'zine *Swish*, for instance, deals exclusively with gay (primarily white) punk rockers, while *Thing* focuses on gay African American drag queens. There is no pretense that there is "something for everyone" here, no delusion that this is for or about "most people" or "everyone" (claims made by most of the mainstream publications, despite the fact that they are just as exclusive and limited as any of the 'zines are). As each, 'zine irreversibly invokes a queer specificity, so the 'zines' multiple voices illustrate that "queer" is not one thing. They smash the myth of "the gay community."

The opposition between "queer" and "lesbian/gay," as created and articulated in the 'zines, as well as in recent political debate and theoretical work, turns on several significantly divergent conceptions of history, identity, and political action. Since the genders of queers are unspecified, and their sexualities only vaguely defined, "queer" does not rely on the homosexual/heterosexual and male/female binarisms that inform lesbianness and gayness, as these subject positions are gendered and opposed to heterosexuality; since queer politics explicitly speaks to, for, and from bisexuality, transsexuality, and, in many cases, heterosexuality and other sexualities and identities, as well as lesbian and gay sexualities, its focus is on the construction and politicization of (sexual) identities, rather than on their fixity or essential inevitability. This political agenda is suggested in the queer's process of self-naming, signifying the embrace and reclamation of a term, traditionally, of derision. The insistence on the word "queer" is an insistence on difference (the word "queer" itself means odd), as opposed to a liberal humanist rhetoric of assimilation that posits lesbians and gay men as essentially the same as everyone else in order to demand "equal rights." Because queerness is so unstable, and because it foregrounds difference rather than commonality, a queer politics, ideally, would also emphasize its own multiple and fragmented nature (i.e., the difference within itself). It would thus, in the spirit of the 'zines, avoid the misguided quest for fixed, transhistorical, and cross-cultural lesbian and gay identities that has characterized much political rhetoric and academic work conducted under the auspices of "lesbian and gay politics" or "lesbian and gay studies."

The "queer" in queer theory, queer politics, and queer identity, also has the potential to undermine what Foucault referred to as the monarchy of sex (see "End") by pluralizing, dispersing, interrogating, opposing, and fragmenting a politics that is organized solely around sexuality as identity. Because queerness is so slippery to define, often connotes a politicization of identity, and does not depend on a binary opposite for its signifying power (the other of "queer"—the "nonqueer"?—whatever it may be, is no more easily contained than "queer" is), it can problematize the kind of single issue activism that has caused further undelineated lesbian and gay articulations to imbue the categories "lesbian" and "gay" with a default whiteness, middle-classness, and USness.

In her article, "To(o) Queer the Writer—Loca, escritora y chicana," Gloria Anzaldúa contrasts the symbolizing power of the words "lesbian" and "queer":

"lesbian" is a cerebral word, white and middle class, representing an English-only dominant culture, derived from the Greek word *lesbos*. I think of lesbians as predominantly white and middle class women and a segment of women of color who acquired the term through osmosis much the same as Chicanas and Latinas assimilated the word "Hispanic." When a "lesbian" names me the same as her she subsumes me under her category. I am of her group but not as an equal part, not as a whole person—my color erased, my class ignored. *Soy una puta mala*, a

phrase coined by Ariban, a *tejana tortillera*. . . . Unlike the word "queer,"
"lesbian" came late into some of our lives. (249–50)

Although she expresses reservations about the word "queer," too, particularly in its embodiment in a white queer theory that seeks to unify queers
or appropriate queers of color, Anzaldúa argues that the historically non-
genteel connotations of "queer" give more room to maneuver its definitionary
parameters.

In the remainder of this essay I explore the uses that Anzaldúa puts
queerness to, primarily in her book *Borderlands/La Frontera: The New Mestiza*,
published in 1987, before "queer" gained its current academic chicness, yet
presaging many of the concerns of queer theory (though Anzaldúa seldom
gets credit when queer theory's lineage is traced or practitioners delineated).
Whereas what are by now ritual analogies between homophobia and racism
interchange whiteness and gayness so that queers of color disappear and gayness bolsters white supremacy across imperial divides, the kinds of racial and
sexual exchanges effected by Anzaldúa centralize queers of color by inter-
pellating queerness from coloredness in a context that explicitly politicizes
queerness as an anti-imperialist and anti-racist (anti-)identity. This is not to
say that Anzaldúa uncritically posits a utopic ethnic or racial identity as a
counterpoint to whiteness and gayness—she is as impatient with Mexican
and Chicano nationalism as she is critical of white arrogance and skeptical of
identitarianism itself—but that her oscillation between discourses of race and
sexuality models a politicized, empowering, and non-idealistic elaboration of
queer race. Anzaldúa's text is multitopical; in this essay I primarily examine
her uses of queerness in it. By focusing on the anti-racist critique of the articulation of a homogenous "lesbian and gay community," I hope to show how the
work of Anzaldúa develops the kinds of arguments suggested in the 'zines,
both in her exemplarization of a colored queer identity and in her fracturing
of all kinds of communities.

In her article "Inverts and Hybrids: Lesbian Rewritings of Sexual and Racial Identities" in the anthology *The Lesbian Postmodern*, Judith Raiskin argues
that Anzaldúa reworks nineteenth and early twentieth century scientific and
sexological discourses bolstering teleologies of racial decadence with reference to categories of sexual perversion, and vice versa, by constructing mestiza and queer subjectivities as privileged consciousnesses. I want to extend
the implications of Raiskin's analysis by suggesting that what Anzaldúa's
work achieves is not merely an inversion of hierarchies (from queer/mestiza =
degenerate to queer/mestiza = transcendent), but also a reconceptualization of
the relationship of the categories to each other and of the ways in which meaning is assigned to and between categorizations.

Anzaldúa begins the Preface to *Borderlands/La Frontera* by initiating a complex relationality between the physical and the psychical, the historical and
the metaphysical, the context-specific and the universal, that will inform the
entire book in various transformations, substitutions, and displacements of
the "original" relation, itself a homologization of abstractions and concretiza-
tions of different registers and media:

The actual physical borderland that I'm dealing with in this book is the Texas–U.S. Southwest/Mexican border. The psychological borderlands, the sexual borderlands and the spiritual borderlands are not particular to the Southwest. In fact, the Borderlands are physically present wherever two or more cultures edge each other, where people of different races occupy the same territory, where under, lower, middle and upper classes touch, where the space between two individuals shrinks with intimacy.

Anzaldúa's opening two sentences establish a contrast enforced in the formal division of labor between their symmetry: the first invokes the specific, the historical, the political, and the material (the Texas–U.S. Southwest/Mexican border); the second gestures toward the "universal," although its inclusion of "sexual borderlands" also suggests more explicitly the kinds of sensual confrontations evoked by the first sentence. The final sentence of the paragraph further unsettles the binary, elaborating the framing imputation that each meaning of the borderland is to be seen as standing for all its other meanings: if the universal and the historically specific inform each other to such a degree that the one cannot mean without the other, then each has been indelibly inf(l)ected to the extent that it immediately brings the other to mind and, as such, has undergone a transformation of its own (particular) meaning. The beginning of the third sentence, "In fact, the Borderlands are physically present wherever two or more cultures edge each other," retrieves the geography of the first sentence to emphasize it in the second: the psychological, sexual, and spiritual borderlands that are not particular to the Southwest are yet as physically present as is the geographic border between Mexico and the United States. Here Anzaldúa's text invites us to break down the borders between the physical and the abstract, to see the latter informed and contextualized by the former.

I have discussed this opening paragraph of *Borderlands/La Frontera* in some detail because of the pattern it establishes for the book as a whole, and, specifically, because of the model it implies for thinking about racial identity, sexual identity, and racialized queerness. By inviting us to transpose our knowledges and understandings in one realm to another apparently unconnected and alien one of a very different order, Anzaldúa displaces and defers any final or single meaning from a particular identification, and, indeed, from identity itself and imbues each identifying moment with particular new meanings as a result of the transpositions.

In the last paragraph of the book's preface, Anzaldúa discusses the language "code switching" in the text and the position of "Chicano Spanish" as a language "not approved by any society" (as she later explains, it is reviled both by Spanish speaking purists and racist English speaking monolinguals). She concludes,

[W]e Chicanos no longer feel that we need to beg entrance, that we need always to make the first overture—to translate to Anglos, Mexicans and Latinos, apology blurting out of our mouths with every step. Today we ask to be met halfway. This book is our invitation to you—from the new mestizas.

I am particularly interested in Anzaldúa's use of gendering and racing pronouns and noun endings in this sentence, again because her strategy here is paradigmatic of a process of (anti-) identity formation/dissolution and a series of transferences and switches that pattern the entire text, but that Anzaldúa never explicitly discusses when she does mention code switchings and cross-identifications. In the sentence cited above, the enclosing "Chicanos" and "mestizas" appear to be synonymous in their identification of the "our" and the "we" that makes "you" of Anglos, Mexicans, and Latinos (in itself an uneasy opposition that fractures the conventionalized white/nonwhite duality). But there is also a teleological transformation in the course of the sentence, as the generic masculine (the conventionalized universal) "Chicanos" becomes what is to be an unconventional universal in the text that follows, the feminine "mestizas," paralleling the shift from upper case nationalism to lower case hybridity/bastardization. Not only, as we shall see, does Anzaldúa's mestiza reflect the anti-identitarian, anti-nationalistic potential of the Queer Nation, but as "queer" comes to stand for "mestiza" in the text, so the metamorphosis into the mestiza also traces the transformation/ (re)definition of the queer and marks the paradoxical nature of the writing-into-being of both identities and trans-substantiations (as the moniker "Queer Nation" itself points to the paradox of an anti-categorical nationalism[3]).

The feminist politics of Anzaldúa's project shapes her transgender identifications and appropriations. Anzaldúa's development of a female universal might be explained with reference to Wittig and Zeig's perverse feminization of classical heroes in *Lesbian Peoples: Materials for a Dictionary* or Wittig's elaboration of conflict and fragmentation within a female universality in *The Lesbian Body*. *Lesbian Peoples* does not carry an entry for "man," and the entry for "woman" notes, "Obsolete since the beginning of the Glorious Age" (165). Using *Lesbian Peoples* to gloss *The Lesbian Body*, we might say that Wittig's universal woman, then, is not so much a separatist being as a transformed separatist; men are not dead, but have been incorporated into the generic she in a reversal of the myth of the gender-neutral he—a reversal both in the sense of a change in political value and in the usurpation of/in gender hierarchies.

In Anzaldúa's book the new universal is further specified by race, but, characteristically of this text, the racialization works not merely to emphasize a binary (racial, ethnic, and linguistic difference is called on to distinguish mestizas and Chicanos from Anglos, Mexicans, and Latinos, rather than to distinguish mestizas from Chicanos), but to multiply its terms and poles. In one of the poems in the latter part of her book, Anzaldúa writes of her role of dragging integrity out of those who engage with her. Her narrator describes how she is repeatedly chosen to "pick at the masks" of "Colored, poor white, latent queer / passing for white" (171). The process of substitution here not only suggests a continuity between "colored," "poor white," and "latent queer," but also makes "poor white" and "latent queer" as much the subject of "passing for white" as "colored" is. How does a latent queer or poor white pass for white? How does one even begin to discover/construct a meaning out of this possibility? Other than simply finding experiences of class, race, and sexuality to be analogous, or seeing all the terms of identity here as highly metaphorical (readings which I am not inclined to follow, and which I do not believe would be amenable to Anzaldúa, either, as will become apparent later), one has to think of these terms as carrying enlarged meanings: class is raced and sexualized; sexuality must carry racial content, as race implies sexuality; and so on.

The "new language—the language of the Borderlands" that Anzaldúa invokes in her preface, refers, then, to more than the English/Spanish linguistic border, or even the boundaries between various Spanish and English languages, dialects, and registers; it also describes a new way of (un)gendering language, and of thinking through the meanings of race, gender, and sexuality. In the section of *Borderlands/La Frontera* entitled "How to Tame a Wild Tongue," Anzaldúa quotes Melanie Kaye/Kantrowitz: "My fingers / move sly against your palm / Like women everywhere we speak in code" (59). This quotation is surrounded by Anzaldúa's discussion of the ways in which Chicano (Anzaldúa uses the masculine ending) culture and speech have historically been punished, marginalized, and misnamed. The insertion of the lines from Kaye/Kantrowitz acts as an intervention into one-dimensional political history by suggesting additional meanings of "women" and "code" here, not only by paralleling lesbian invisibility with Chicana and Chicano marginalization, but also by deploying race and gender metonymically to stand for one another, so that transcategorical intertextuality and interpretation becomes itself an extension of the queer's penchant for cross-identifying and eluding identity. In his *Making Things Perfectly Queer: Interpreting Mass Culture*, Alexander Doty suggests that the exemplary queer identification is cross-identification (a gay man making a lesbian identification, a straight man making a gay male identification, etc.). Anzaldúa's queer methodology constructs cross-identifications between race and gender and, as we shall see, between race and sexuality. She uses queerness to make queer identifications, to make identification queer, and to queer identity.

Anzaldúa draws a parallel between queers and mestizas in making the provocative claim that all marginalized peoples are mestizas (Lectures), and in her discussion of what she calls "a mestiza consciousness" (*Borderlands* 80). She says that as mestizas cross all kinds of borders, so queers exist in every culture and yet are also outcasts in each one. Anzaldúa thus formulates a politicized queer identity, using "queer" to denote oppositionality (in striking contrast to the proposition, encouraged by many mainstream activist groups, that lesbians and gay men are "just like everyone else") and to establish analogies with other marginal identities when she writes of the borderlands between the United States and Mexico, between and within cultures, between genders, genres, languages, and within the self,

> The prohibited and forbidden are its inhabitants. *Los atravesados* live here: the squint-eyed, the perverse, the queer, the troublesome, the mongrel, the mulatto, the half-breed, the half dead; in short, those who cross over, pass over, or go through the confines of the "normal." (3)[4]

Anzaldúa disperses the category "queer" so that it resists the kind of appropriations that white lesbians and gay men might want to make in order to

conform Anzaldúa to their own fixed lesbian and gay (and even queer) precon-
ceptions. Anzaldúa's queerness also returns to the radical politics of the first
lesbian and gay activists in the United States and Europe and prefigures contemporary "queer" politics by, for instance, reclaiming the "berdache" tradition
of some native American cultures. Rather than assimilating into hegemonic de-
lineations of gender (i.e., dualistic prescriptions of appropriate maleness and
femaleness), as is the wont amongst more conservative lesbians and gay men in
the United States, she describes the border inhabitant as "forerunner of a new
race, / half and half—both woman and man, neither— / a new gender" (194).

Out of its context, Anzaldúa's metaphorization of mestiza identity could
authorize a colonizing appropriation: those white lesbians and gay men, for
example, who are already overly eager to claim that, because they suffer from
(homophobic) discrimination they "know what it feels like" to be a person of
color, might feel encouraged to conflate these very different kinds of oppression
and so to avoid having to recognize and confront their own racism and to own
their own inevitable imbrication in racist power structures. Anzaldúa might be
seen as inviting the renewed erasure of the voices, bodies, and lives of mestizas
by, in the name of anti-essentialism and alliance-building, apparently legitimat-
ing a following of white lesbians and gay men identifying as mestizas. In *Bor-
derlands/La Frontera* she makes a similar universalizing claim for "queer":

> As a *mestiza* I have no country, my homeland cast me out; yet all coun-
> tries are mine because I am every woman's sister or potential lover. (As
> a lesbian I have no race, my own people disclaim me; but I am all races
> because there is the queer of me in all races.) (80)[5]

Her postulation that she is all races because there is the queer of her in all races
would be suspect if made from a white perspective or from within a Western
history. However, her metaphoric mestiza speaks clearly from an experience
and radical understanding of sexism, racism, and U.S. imperialism. She thus
frames the queer's claim as a multi-layered one. Not only does she situate
Borderlands/La Frontera within a feminist perspective and Mexican, Mexican-
American, and Chicana/Chicano history and suffuse the text with references
and allusions to a mestiza/o and (female) Indian cultural heritage, but she also
embodies her anti-Eurocentrism in the actual language of her book by extensively using various forms of English and Spanish in it, as well as smatterings
of Nahuatl. These features of lived experience and commitments to a contesta-
tory politics cannot be analogized or transferred onto a bland white identity
the way that "multiculturalism" in its popular invocation in the United States
has erased the materiality of political conflict by skimming culture off the top
of the work and lives of people of color.[6]

The essays that comprise the first half of *Borderlands/La Frontera* chronicle
genocide against Native Americans, the history of U.S. imperialism in Mexico,
the lynchings of Mexicans in the United States, and the development of various institutions of exploitation and racism like the *maquiladores* on the U.S.-
Mexican border. These frames ensure that Anzaldúa's dissolutions of identity

and multiplications of signification achieve their effect precisely because they are working from within an already established network of experiential and political affiliations. They, in fact, rely on the very knowledges that they work to undo and, as such, are not synonymous with attacks on these identities emanating from a racist, sexist, or homophobic politics.[7] Anzaldúa explains this point of departure in terms of her contestation of hegemonic cultural norms, but it is equally true of her processes of undermining and resignifying identity/identities per se: "I feel perfectly free to rebel and to rail against my culture. I fear no betrayal on my part because, unlike Chicanas and other women of color who grew up white or who have only recently returned to their native cultural roots, I was totally immersed in mine" (21).

The later essays and many of the poems that make up the second half of the volume treat what by convention are more metaphysical concerns (the exploration of a disavowed part of the self), but these concerns come to be indelibly political (as metaphors and as themselves) as they are politically constructed by the histories that contextualize them in the book's opening sections. As Kate Adams points out, Anzaldúa's framing of her poetry in *Borderlands/La Frontera* is fairly unique: contemporary poetry is almost always published in chap book form or as part of a poetry anthology. The elaborate preface to the poetry (Adams notes that Anzaldúa originally conceived of the book as a ten-page prose preface preceding a volume of poetry, rather than the present 200 pages equally divided between essays and poetry) politicizes the poems in much the same way that the political histories delineated by Anzaldúa foreclose a pluralistic reading of her queers or mestizas or queer(/)mestizas.[8]

Anzaldúa's contexts thus function in contradictory ways in the book. For while they serve to establish the text's anti-racist and anti-imperialist politics and to ground her formulation of mestiza and queer subjects, they also become the objects of the motif of self-critique and subject-dissolution that shapes the book's structure and thematics. Anzaldúa explains that her "Chicana identity is grounded in the Indian woman's history of resistance" (21): that tradition of resistance is transposable across cultures and identifications, so that, finally and ironically, it is also the grounds for a resistance to the grounds itself, to itself. Anzaldúa refuses to reify any single/singular identity: just as the mestiza will demand the recognition of all her heritages, and the queer will traverse and inhabit all of these heritages, so Anzaldúa will not give into cultural purists or univocal nationalists who want her to "return" to a uncontaminated Mexican past; she insists on her "Americanness" also. She insistently claims the English language, too. She isn't satisfied with any stable identity. Perhaps the most courageous and empowering facet of the book is Anzaldúa's refusal to idealize any mythically good Indian past or Chicano present. She critiques the historical and contemporary sexism and homophobia in the cultures which find their confluence in her body and experience at the same time that she indicts white racism and U.S. imperialism: "But I will not glorify those aspects of my culture which have injured me and which have injured me in the name of protecting me" (22). Yet, rather than lamenting her own homelessness/statelessness/non-identity as a Chicana lesbian who feels excluded from her homophobic and sexist Chicano home and persecuted by the racist culture of her geographical homeland, her text becomes a bitter-sweet celebration of bastardization, of the richness of her border queer-mestiza identity.

As a literary text, *Borderlands/La Frontera* further shatters any notion of identity as unitary, fixed, stable, or comfortable in its resistance to the categories of genre that inform traditional English courses and the disciplinary demarcations that constitute academic institutions in general. It seems to encompass, for instance, poetry, theory, autobiography, mythology, criticism, narrative, history, and political science, while suggesting the limitations of these delimitations and, ultimately, of delimitation itself. Rather than substituting one identity for another, then, Anzaldúa's text presents a fundamental critique and reformulation of the very notion of identity, albeit—crucially—from a politicized Chicana lesbian perspective.

Anzaldúa's text explodes the categories "America" and "American literature," too. The extent to which her book challenges English literary canons was illustrated to me by student evaluations of a course on "Modern American Fiction" in which I taught *Borderlands/La Frontera*. One student, for instance, when asked to comment on the readings that I selected for the course, wrote, "hate [David] Wojnarowicz, did not like reading Anzaldúa because I only speak English, [Robert] Coover was great." A later question on the evaluation form asked "What was most valuable about this course? What recommendations would you make for improvement? Use the space below for your comments." The same student responded, "I don't think you should need to understand Spanish to read a book in a Modern American Fiction course." This student's ethnocentric conception of what constitutes "Modern American Fiction" is a reflection of hegemonic constructions of literary canons in educational institutions and of efforts by conservative political figures to mobilize racist, sexist, classist, and homophobic prejudices in the service of a monolithic "American culture" (with its English only family values). The irony, of course, is that it is these blinkered views that constitute the true "American fiction," while Anzaldúa's text is a representative analysis par excellence of contemporary U.S. cultures and experiences and, in fact, can be seen as an exemplary instance of U.S. culture. Her new mestiza is the archetypal American. I should also add that one of the Chicana students in the class (although the written evaluations were anonymous, I am assuming that the above response was written by a white student) appeared to be equally offended by Anzaldúa's book, not because it used Spanish, but because of the "poor" Spanish and "bad words" that the student felt Anzaldúa used. The student explained that she had been taught not to "speak like that"; she felt that Anzaldúa's text was disgracing Chicanas and Chicanos.

Finally, Anzaldúa's book eludes hegemonic paradigms of reading and teaching in the academic institutions and disciplines that are now starting to teach and study it. In a 1987 article on "Intelligibility and Meaningfulness in Multicultural Literature in English," Reed Way Dasenbrock argued that what he referred to as "multicultural" writers like Maxine Hong Kingston and Rudolfo Anaya used specific rhetorical strategies in their texts to bridge the gaps between their various constituencies of readers. Commenting specifically on the problems that a monolingual reader might have with these texts, as compared to a bilingual-bicultural reader, and the calculated disconcertions that writers feed these monocultural readers, Dasenbrock nevertheless concluded, "No matter where one starts, the difference between the two reading experiences should be eliminated or at least reduced by the books' ends, as the monocultural reader should be that much less monocultural than at the start" (16). I want to reconfigure Dasenbrock's thesis in order to apply it to Anzaldúa's book and to suggest that *Borderlands/La Frontera*, also published in 1987, actually goes even further in its construction and confounding of a multiple readership. Not only does the text undermine the kind of us/them dichotomy implied in Dasenbrock's analysis by positing an apparently infinite number of identities and constituencies in its possible audience, thus bypassing any impetus to pander to the perplexities of a white readership that is constituted in binary opposition to a readership of color, but it also doesn't seem to move toward resolution, reconciliation, truth, or knowledge for any of those readerships (as neither my white student nor my Chicana student felt that the book spoke sufficiently closely to their own experience).

No matter how many historical contexts any reader knows or studies, complete mastery of this text will always be elusive. As one reads Anzaldúa's book, it becomes apparent that it needs to be understood within specific contexts, but each context in turn suggests others. Because the identities that Anzaldúa elaborates resist stabilization, there is no bottom line context that reveals a final truth. Context is infinite. *Borderlands/La Frontera* intersects with many histories: Chicana/o history requires an understanding of Mexican/U.S. relations, an understanding that in turn points to Mexican history, a history that, in turn, invites an examination of Latin American history as a whole, and so on; Chicana/o history also intersects with the history of the labor movement in the United States, and with Chicana feminism, and white feminism; Anzaldúa's queerness is intricated within the struggle for lesbian and gay rights, and with a specifically Chicana/o lesbian and gay history, and so on. And so on.

Anzaldúa's text explicitly demonstrates what poststructuralist theorists have been arguing for three decades: there can be no mastery of a text, there can be no all-knowing teacher. No single reader will be able to "understand" every addressed identity of *Borderlands/La Frontera*: a heterosexual Chicana might feel excluded from the queer identity elaborated in the text; a white lesbian might feel alienated from the book's mestiza consciousness or its use of Spanish; a Chicana lesbian who does speak Spanish and English might find some of Anzaldúa's specific border colloquialisms unintelligible. Because Anzaldúa deploys so many kinds and registers of Spanish and Spanish-English mixtures in the text, as well as English and Nahuatl, most bilingual readers are frustrated by one or another moment in the book. Understanding is always partial and fragmented. While it is important for us to do our homework/research, it is also important that as readers we stop feeling frustrated because of our inability to understand everything in the text, and that as teachers we undermine impetuses to present ourselves as all-knowing. We need to emphasize that it's okay not to have access to everything in a text, that, in fact, it is worthwhile for teachers and students to recognize and cultivate and become comfortable with this partiality and fragmentation. This might be the best lesson in identity, politics, and difference that we can teach and learn.

I have already mentioned the contradictory way in which Anzaldúa uses her various heritages to provide a counter-identity to the values of Anglo-America: she deploys these apparently stable identities to critique racism and imperialism, but also destabilizes and deconstructs these enabling grounds of counter-identification as she finds identity itself more and more elusive. She both defends and criticizes "her" culture in a series of gestures that establish the elliptical trajectory of *Borderlands/La Frontera*. The entire book seems to be at odds with itself as it mourns the loss of a putative wholeness[9] and seeks to overcome division, while also recognizing the inevitability of this multivocality and even celebrating fragmentation as the enabling scene of the mestiza consciousness that Anzaldúa advocates. At times the voice in the text seems to long for a unity that implies an essentialist and nostalgic understanding of human subjectivity and history[10] and, specifically, to insist on the singularity and homogeneity of "the Mexican way of life" (10) and "the Mexican culture" (48). Yet we are shown equally insistently that "There is no one Chicano language just as there is no one Chicano experience" (58). The movement from "Mexican" to "Chicano" represents not only an ethnic, historical, and political rupture/evolution, but also a refiguring of the terms of subjectivity: contradiction, hybridization, and transposition to replace continuity and identity.

No sooner has the narrator informed us of her quest to find her "own intrinsic nature buried under the personality that had been imposed on" her than she asserts, "Culture forms our beliefs" (16), as if to deny that any such beliefless "intrinsic" nature exists. She disabuses us of our utopian impulse to retrieve a matriarchal historical originality by pointing to the hegemonic patriarchal ideologies of pre-Columbian America (5), only to locate a foundational gender symmetry in early Aztec society (31, 33). While the Shadow-Beast of her/our fears seems to be an essentialist being who signals our "true" selves that have been repressed, and who might break out of its cage and shatter our masks of conformity (20), in the more explicitly concretized realm of racial power relations, "The only 'legitimate' inhabitants are those in power, the whites *and those who align themselves with whites*" (3–4; emphasis added)— where we might expect an essentialist demarcation, we find that race breaks down in the shifting sands of political affiliation.

Borderlands/La Frontera is enabled precisely by contradictory movements such as these, and I believe we would be missing the originality of Anzaldúa's vision were we to see them as weaknesses in her argument.[11] Instead, I read these movements as complementing the kinds of switches, transferals, and dissolutions that I have been elaborating, since they elude the epistemological and political linearity that hypostatizes a final or bottom line identity (either as resistance or as domination) and question our very understandings and articulations of identity and processes of identification. Judith Raiskin and Inderpal Grewal have suggested that Anzaldúa's work combines political commitment with a postmodern critique of identity. Thus the tensions between Anzaldúa's reclamation of a non-sexist pre-Aztec Indian heritage and her critique of the unified subject would testify to her adept negotiations between the insights of poststructuralist theory and the political and epistemological claims of communities devalued by patriarchal values and Western imperialism and racism.

I think we can further understand these and other "inconsistencies" in the book as more than the clash of a politically strategic essentialism with a skepticism of humanist ideologies, because they also invite us to reformulate our understandings of and responses to notions of contradiction and ambiguity. In the section of *Borderlands/La Frontera* entitled *"La herencia de Coatlicue/The Coatlicue* State," Anzaldúa writes that *Coatlicue*, the Serpent goddess who was divided and disempowered by a male-dominated Azteca-Mexica culture (27),

> depicts the contradictory. In her figure, all the symbols important to the religion and philosophy of the Aztecs are integrated. Like Medusa, the Gorgon, she is a symbol of the fusion of opposites: the eagle and the serpent, heaven and the underworld, life and death, mobility and immobility, beauty and horror. (47)

Later she writes of the new mestiza consciousness that is flexible and plural, and that tolerates ambiguity and contradiction (79–80). This ambiguity extends to the very nature and role of the new mestiza herself. While she may resolve ambivalence (79), she does not resolve contradictions. She is not ambivalent about contradiction: her charge is to keep "breaking down the unitary aspect of each new paradigm" (80), but also to heal the splits in our lives, cultures, and languages (80). She is attempting to fragment paradigms and proliferate contradiction, even as she multiplies her own contradictory imbrications in the apparatuses of contradiction—this is what it means to live in the borderlands/*la frontera*.

I have tried to show how the logic of *Borderlands/La Frontera* works to dismantle categorizations and derail predictable outcomes, both in the delineation of a new kind of consciousness and in the actual structure and vocabulary of the book. This process functions at all the levels of identity formulated in the text and shapes the articulation of queer race: a politicizing slippage between the marks of race and queerness that racializes queerness and queers race in the body, in the meetings of bodies, and in the theorizations of these bodies and meetings. The demarcations of race and sexuality are ultimately reinvented to such an extent that they are torn from their conventional meanings and reworked into an inextricable, mutually dependent, mutually informing, yet polysignifying cluster of meanings and associations, both intimately material and infinitely metaphorical.

Anzaldúa's text invites us to generate reading strategies that are as synchronically multivalent as are its own structures and embodiments. It articulates a queer *mestisaje* at the same time that it destabilizes both terms through each other. We, as readers, in turn, have to re-understand the terms through the contexts Anzaldúa sets up, while also absorbing their anti-homophobic and anti-racist originating agendas. *Borderlands/La Frontera* provides a model for queer theory of how to delineate the pluperfect sexualization of racial identities and racialization of sexual identities without prioritizing either identity or losing the force and particularity of an anti-homophobic or anti-racist critique, but thereby destabilizes the identity of queer theory itself. The book also destabilizes racial categories and, by necessary extension, the discipline of ethnic studies, in its metaphorization of ethnicity in order to suture it to an anti-homophobic imperative. For me this paradoxical dialectic resonates with the words of Johnny Noxzema and Rex Boy with which I began this essay, because it describes their own (and my own) very conflicted imbrication in the politics and theory of identity and diversity, while also suggesting the potential for an empowering and productive deployment of this conflict in our readings and writings of a multi-ethnic and multiply ethnic U.S. culture.

Portions of pages 1-3 [65–67] of this essay previously appeared in my article "Queer Zines and the Fragmentation of Art Community Identity Politics" in Socialist Review. *I thank the* Socialist Review *editorial collective for permission to reprint that material here. In addition, I thank the following for assisting me with this article: Mónica Szurmuk, Holly Bauer, Juan Corona, Margarita Barceló, Adriana Novoa, Anne Shea, Javier Morillo-Alicea, and Sheryl Gobble.*

NOTES

1. For some brief histories and analyses of the queer 'zine phenomenon, see Freeman and Berlant, Botkin, Freilicher, "'Zines," Mindich, Fenster and Viegener. An extensive annotated queer 'zine bibliography appears as *Queer Zine Explosion*, published about twice a year.

2. Spew is the name of an annual 'zine "convention."

3. See Bérubé and Escoffier.

4. When quoting from *Borderlands/La Frontera*, I have followed the text's use of italics.

5. See also page 84: "Being the supreme crossers of cultures, homosexuals have strong bonds with the queer white, Black, Asian, Native American, Latino, and with the queer in Italy, Australia and the rest of the planet."

6. See Gomez-Pefia, Dev.

7. For further discussion of this paradoxical strategy of deconstructing identity from within a politics of identity, in the context of affiliations of gender and sexual orientation, see my "Macho Sluts" and "Queer Fictions."

8. For further discussion of the problematic of pluralism in relation to Anzaldúa's text, see Lugones.

9. For instance, Anzaldúa writes of the Mexico/U.S. border,

> 1,950 mile-long open wound
> dividing a *pueblo,* a culture,
> running down the length of my body,
> staking fence rods in my flesh,
> splits me splits me *me raja me raja.* (2)

10. For example, Anzaldúa blames Western culture for splitting the brain and reality into two functions (psychic and material) (37).

11. Annamarie Jagose, for one, criticizes Anzaldúa for contradicting herself in the book (138, 152).

WORKS CITED

Adams, Kate. "Northamerican Silences: History, Identity, and Witness in the Poetry of Gloria Anzaldúa, Cherríe Moraga, and Leslie Marmon Silko." *Listening to Silences: New Essays in Feminist Criticism.* Ed. Elaine Hedges and Shelley Fisher Fishkin. New York: Oxford UP, 1994. 130–45.

Anzaldúa, Gloria E. *Borderlands/La Frontera: The New Mestiza.* San Francisco: Aunt Lute, 1987.

———. Lectures Ethnic Studies Program. U of California. San Diego, 21–22 May 1990.

———. "To(o) Queer the Writer—Loca, escritora y chicana." *Versions: Writing by Dykes, Queers & Lesbians.* Ed. Betsy Warland. Vancouver: Press Gang, 1991. 249–63.

Barnard, Ian. "Queer Fictions: Gay Men With/And/In/Near/Or Lesbian Feminisms?" *LIT: Literature, Interpretation, Theory* 4.4 (1993): 261–74.

———. "Macho Sluts: Genre-Fuck, S/M Fantasy, and the Reconfiguration of Political Action." *Genders* 19 (1994): 265–91.

Bérubé, Allan, and Jeffrey Escoffier. "Queer/Nation." *Out/Look* 11 (Winter 1991): 12–14.

Botkin, Michael C. "Behind the Zines." *Bay Area Reporter* 17 Sept. 1992: 11.

Brownworth, Victoria A. "The Porn Boom." *Lesbian News* 18.7 (1993): 42+.

Cooper, Dennis. "Queercore." *The Village Voice* 30 June 1992: 31–33.

Dasenbrock, Reed Way. "Intelligibility and Meaningfulness in Multicultural Literature in English." *PMLA* 102.1 (Jan. 1987): 10–19.

Dev, Elango. "Cultural Diversity and the Politics of Assimilation." *New Indicator* 28:1, 7.

Doty, Alexander. *Making Things Perfectly Queer: Interpreting Mass Culture.* Minneapolis: U of Minnesota P, 1993.

Fenster, Mark. "Queer Punk Fanzines: Identity, Community, and The Articulation of Homosexuality and Hardcore." *Journal of Communication Inquiry* 17.1 (1993): 73–94.

Foucault, Michel. "The End of the Monarchy of Sex." 1977. *Foucault Live: Interviews, 1966–84.* Ed. Sylvère Lotringer. Trans. John Johnston. New York: Semiotext(e), 1989. 137–55.

Freeman, Elizabeth, and Lauren Berlant. "Queer Nationality." *boundary 2* 19.1 (Spring 1992): 149–80.

Freilicher, Mel. "Fight the Power: *Diseased Pariah News,* etc." *Fiction International* 22 (1992): 177–85.

Gomez-Peña, Guillermo. "The Multicultural Paradigm: An Open Letter to the National Arts Community." *High Performance* Fall 1989: 18–27.

Grewal, Inderpal. "Autobiographic Subjects and Diasporic Locations: *Meatless Days* and *Borderlands.*" *Scattered Hegemonies: Postmodernity and Transnational Feminist Practices.* Ed. Inderpal Grewal and Caren Kaplan. Minneapolis: U of Minnesota P, 1994. 231–54.

Holy Titclamps 9 (Winter 91–92).

Holy Titclamps Zine Explosion 3 (February 1992).

Jagose, Annamarie. "Slash and Suture: The Border's Figuration of Colonialism, Phallocentrism, and Homophobia in *Borderlands/La Frontera: The New Mestiza.*" *Lesbian Utopics.* New York: Routledge, 1994. 137–57.

Lugones, María. "On *Borderlands/La Frontera:* An Interpretive Essay." *Hypatia* 7.4 (1992): 31–37.

Mindich, Jeremy. "Soap Box Samurai." *Details* Aug. 1993: 96–101.

Raiskin, Judith "Inverts and Hybrids: Lesbian Rewritings of Sexual and Racial Identities." *The Lesbian Postmodern.* Ed. Laura Doan. New York: Columbia UP, 1994. 156–72.

Salvador, Christian. "Queer Generations." *Infected Faggot Perspectives* 11 (Sept./Oct. 1992): 8–9.

Viegener, Matias. "Queer Lettres." *American Book Review* 14.4 (1992): 3+.

———. "There's Trouble in That Body: Queer Fanzines, Sexual Identity and Censorship." *Fiction International* 22 (1992): 123–36.

Wittig, Monique. *The Lesbian Body.* 1973. Trans. David Le Vay. Boston: Beacon, 1986.

Wittig, Monique, and Sande Zeig. *Lesbian Peoples: Material for a Dictionary.* New York: Avon, 1979.

"'Zines, Queens and Everything in Between: Fear and Loathing in Chicago." *Homoture* 3: n.p.

Sandra Cisneros: Form over Content

Ilan Stavans

Officially anointed *La Girlfriend* by the English-speaking media, Sandra Cisneros is considered a living classic. She is the most sought-after Latina writer of her generation and a guest impossible to ignore in any multicultural fiesta. The black-and-white photographs used to promote her work are colored by an overwhelming sense of theatricality. They make her look like a sweet light-skinned Indian with a European flair—a natural beauty out of a Sergei Eisenstein film. Her enigmatic smile hides the ancient mysteries of her people, and her cowboy boots, tiny miniskirts, idiosyncratic Mexican shawls, and hairbands inject the needed exoticism into her ethnic roots.*

Her status as the voice of a minority has not befallen by accident. Born in 1954 in a Chicago barrio and educated in the Midwest, Cisneros acquired her distinct *tejano* identity when she settled in San Antonio in the mid-eighties. She has since turned the U.S.–Mexican border into her habitat. She proudly parades around under a hybrid facade, part nativist Spanish and part anti-establishment American. She is constantly asking her audience to approach her as the star of a cross-cultural *bildungsroman* where *mestizas*, ignored and underrepresented for ages, end up baking the cake and eating it all. Indeed, Cisneros describes herself as "nobody's wife and nobody's mother" and "an informal spokeswoman for Latinos." Her imposed profile is that of an eternal sympathizer of lost causes, a loose woman, a south-of-the-border feminist outlaw happily infuriating anyone daring to obstruct her way. "They say I'm a bitch," a poem of hers reads,

> Or witch. I've claimed
> the same and never winced.

First published in *Academic Questions* 9, 4 (Fall 1996). Reprinted in *The Riddle of Cantinflas: Essays on Hispanic Popular Culture* (Albuquerque, NM: University of New Mexico Press, 1998).

* I examine Sandra Cisneros in the context of Latino culture in *The Hispanic Condition.*

They say I'm a *macha*, hell on wheels,
viva-la-vulva, fire and brimstone
man-hating, devastating,
boogey-woman lesbian.
Not necessarily,
but I like the compliment.

By all accounts I am
a danger to society.
I'm Pancha Villa.
I break laws
upset the natural order,
anguish the Pope and make fathers cry.
I am beyond the jaw of law.
I'm *la desperada*, most-wanted public enemy.
My happy picture grinning from the wall.

Her artistic talents are clear but overemphasized. In fact, what truly attracts readers is not her compact prose, which she perceives as "English with a Spanish sensibility," but her nasty, taboo-breaking attitude. Her works are pamphleteering. They denounce rather than move; they accuse rather than educate.

Responsible for several poetry collections, a children's book, and a couple of volumes of fiction, Cisneros hit high into the firmament with her 1984 novel *The House on Mango Street*, a chain of interrelated vignettes widely read from coast to coast and repeatedly assigned to undergraduates. The plot is unified by the voice of Esperanza Cordero, a preteenage girl coming to terms with her impoverished surroundings and her urge to write her life. Cisneros's second published book, with the imprint of Arte Público Press, a small nonprofit house at the University of Houston devoted to minority literature, *The House on Mango Street* came out just as she was celebrating her thirtieth birthday. The match between writer and publisher seemed ideal: a simple, cliché-filled coming-of-age tale by and about Hispanic women, uncomplicated and unapologetic, with the potential for enchanting a broad audience of young school girls, and a federally funded press whose mandate had been to place in bookshelves the fiction by Latinos that mainstream New York publishers refused to endorse. In a short time both parties benefited greatly, the unknown Cisneros becoming, without any major reviews, an incipient version of the *bandida latina* that would later blossom, and her title turning out to be one of the fastest selling in the house's catalogue.

That all happened when diversity and the politics of inclusion were still in diapers. By the late eighties, multiculturalism had become a national obsession, and a spokesfigure for the brewing Latino minority was urgently needed. Richard Rodriguez, whose autobiography *Hunger of Memory* had appeared in 1982, was already an illustrious presence, but his antibilingualism, often confused for anti-Hispanicism, seemed repugnant and xenophobic to the liberal establishment. Since Rodriguez stood alone, an unopposed male, a right-wing intellectual whose soul not even the devil could buy, a female counterpart was quickly sought. Cisneros seized the opportunity: Susan Bergholz, a Manhattan literary agent making a niche for emerging Latinos literati, took her as a client; soon after, Vintage agreed to reprint *The House on Mango Street* and Random House to publish another collection of stories, *Woman Hollering Creek*. A sudden metamorphosis occurred. Talented and outgoing as she was, Cisneros *la marginal* became Cisneros *la atractiva*. With the help of the right promotional machinery, she moved to center stage, and the applause hasn't stopped: From a Before Columbus American Book Award to a MacArthur Fellowship, she basks in the spotlight, sporting fancy sunglasses to reduce the glare.

But the problem, paraphrasing Gore Vidal, is that Cisneros wants to be not good but great, and so she is neither. Her style shows signs of maturity; her tales are not prepubescent anymore, and her sentimentality has mellowed down. *Woman Hollering Creek*, for instance, offers a gamut of pieces of self-discovery, set primarily in southern Texas and Mexico, often overstyled, on the role of women in our collective psyche: Rachel, narrating "Eleven," tells what it is like being a girl of that age; Ines Alfaro, who in "Eyes of Zapata" runs away with Mexican general Emiliano Zapata, talks about how his machismo destroyed her life; Cleófila Enriqueta de León Hernández, the character at the heart of the title story, follows her husband to the United States, where she realizes the extent of her own oppression—to cite only three among many other "suffering souls." These tales are neither fully original nor groundbreaking. Race and gender are their stuff, which Cisneros, by an act of cultural fiat, recycles with just the right ingredients to call attention to Hispanics as instinctual and exciting and interesting. For what they are worth, a handful are actually commendable, but the public has embraced them with far less ardor than it had *The House on Mango Street*, which isn't a good novel. It is sleek and sentimental, sterile and undemanding. Its seductive flavor, I guess, is to be found in its primitiveness. What Cisneros does is tackle important social issues from a peripheral, condescending angle, drawing her readers to the hardship her female characters experience but failing to offer an insightful examination of who they are and how they respond to their environment.

Since its republication by Vintage, *The House on Mango Street* has sold close to a quarter of a million copies. It might seem fine for seventh graders, but making it required reading in high schools and colleges from coast to coast, where students should have more substantial fare, is saddening. Its impact in the United States, obviously, has resonated worldwide. It has appeared in a dozen translations, including the unrefined Spanish one made by Elena Poniatowska, another one of Susan Bergholz's clients and Mexico's most important *femme de lettres*. Cisneros builds her narrative by means of minuscule literary snapshots, occasionally as short as half a page. Esperanza Cordero, whose name in Spanish means "hope," thinks aloud. She describes what she sees and hears in poetic terms, focusing on the women who surround her and the way they are victimized by men. The image of the house, a ubiquitous motif in so-called Third World fiction, becomes the central leitmotif: Esperanza's poor house embarrasses and pains her; she dreams of a larger, embellished one, a signature of the better times she yearns for for herself and her family. Men in her neighborhood are by nature evil; women, on the other hand, particularly the untraditional ones, are saintly, and she seeks a handful of them (Minerva, Alicia, Aunt Guadalupe) as role models. At one point Esperanza is raped as she accompanies her friend Sally to a carnival. At another, Sally is beaten by her father as punishment for seeing boys. The cast is presented as real folks but, in truth, it is Manichean and buffoonish. Together they introduce a risky rhetoric of virtue that utilizes the powerless victim to advance a critique of the Hispanic idiosyncrasy, but that fails to explore any other of its multiple facets.

Cisneros seasons her plot with the type of "magical realism" readers have grown accustomed to in Latin American masterpieces. This is done to make her work ethnic enough; it validates its authenticity. A witch woman, for instance, reads Esperanza's cards to unravel her destiny, and what she finds is "a home in the heart." Her identity quest is dissociated into alternative selves, all related to the various names she dreams of possessing. But her main concern is with the female body. Her descriptions of Esperanza's nascent sexuality are built upon the recognition of the opposite sex as a bestial monster ready to attack. A distant resemblance can be found between Cisneros's novel and Alice Walker's *The Color Purple*. Clearly Walker is much more concerned with relevant historical issues; she tackles slavery from a female perspective and reaches a level of high melodrama as her protagonist, Celie, undergoes a transformation from passive acceptance to self-assertion and human dignity. The epistolary structure of her book, as well as her use of dialect, give it a depth absent in Cisneros. Nonetheless, both writers resort to the same manipulative devices: Their novels depict men within an ethnic minority as patently evil and detail the psychological development of female characters who, only through conversion, can receive redemption. First you learn to understand the injustices of the environment, and then you become your own master.

Does the book deserve its current status? The answer is no. True enough, Latino fiction in English is still green, but turning *The House on Mango Street* into obligatory reading, presumably because of its accessibility, is wrong. It ratifies the image of Hispanics as sentimental dullards, and, equally worrisome, it celebrates the Latino intellectual as pubescent protester. I do not mean to blame Cisneros for a wrong she is not responsible for. Hers is a first novel, a debutante's first turn around the dance floor. What is disturbing is the uncritical deification that surrounds her book. Scholars date the origins of the genre back to 1959, when José Antonio Villarreal published *Pocho*, a tale of revolution and assimilation, about a young Mexican-American kid facing discrimination and finding his rightful place in America. Since then a lot of what is published today by Latino fiction writers is realistic and semiautobiographical. The field is clearly awaiting a major breakthrough that will push its boundaries from conventional immigrant literature to a more sophisticated world-class writing, the type of transition carried on by Philip Roth and Saul Bellow in Jewish letters in the United States. Whenever such reformulating takes place, a recognition of earlier nontraditional voices will be crucial. Few, for instance, regard the pre-postmodern novelistic exercises by an Iberian, Felipe Alfau's *Locos: A Comedy of Gestures*, published in 1936, as a Latino ancestor, if anything because Alfau was a conservative fellow, unconcerned with ethnic envies, and also because, as a Spaniard, he automatically suits the profile of the oppressor. His novel, though, in the line of Pirandello and Italo Calvino, is light-years ahead of the immigrant-handles-it-all fiction we have grown accustomed to by a considerable segment of the Latino intelligentsia.

But the pantheon is vastly expanding, and high-caliber figures like Oscar Hijuelos, Julia Alvarez, Aristeo Brito, and Cristina García have already delivered commanding and mature novels, at once multifaceted and far-reaching, volumes that go far beyond easy stereotypes. Their understanding of what fiction ought to do—an investigation into the obscure aspects of humanity—makes Cisneros, by comparison, a far less demanding artist. Her messages come in soundbites and often have the taste of stale political sloganeering. She makes social protest the foundation for utopia. Trapped in her condition as Hispanic and woman, her creation, Esperanza, can only rely on her words and imagination to escape. She vows not to grow up tame, which makes her perceive poetry as the door out—her way of escape to an alternative life, her device to reject the ugliness of the outside world. So what type of literary model is *La Girlfriend*? Confrontational yet wholeheartedly anti-intellectual, her pen is just a weapon to incriminate. Nothing new in this, of course; after all, Cisneros is part, indirectly at least, of the illustrious genealogy of Latin American writers qua opponents to the system, from Joé Martí to Rosario Castellanos and Elena Poniatowska herself. But her ready-made U.S. odyssey, her "making it" in the American Dream, is curiously harmless. Hers is a domesticated form of belligerence. Rather than position herself as opponent to the powers that be, she courts them, feeds them with the dose of animosity they need, and in turn is fed lavishly by them on a diet of awards and prizes. Her forte lies in her articulation of words, not in her display and knowledge of ideas. She offers neither surprises nor profound explorations of the human spirit. The ethnocentrism that gives her legitimacy transforms her complaints into bourgeois mannerisms—transitory temper tantrums that society is ready to accept simply because they present no real subversive threat. Her tales are flat and unoriginal and thrive on revising moribund stereotypes.

In short, the acclaim granted by the liberal establishment to *The House on Mango Street*, and to this nineties version of the flamboyant Mexican artist Frida Kahlo, as the classic Latina writer of her generation, is, to me at least, a form of collective nearsightedness and one more evidence of how exoticism pays its dues. What forces us to give simplistic, overly accessible novels, fiction cum caricature, to the young? Are they allergic to more complex readings? Or could it be that our research into the archives of Latino literature has not gone far enough? By endorsing Cisneros's attitude and no one else's, the risk of falsifying the role of Latino intellectuals is quite high. All serious literature, by definition, is subversive, but in our MTV age, not all of it needs to be foul-mouthed and lightweight.

PART II
TESTIMONIOS

Between the Milkman and the Fax Machine: Challenges to Women Writers in the Caribbean

Sherezada "Chiqui" Vicioso

Translated by Daisy Cocco De Filippis

My name is Chiqui—not Chico. Vicioso—not Viscoso. And I hang on to my name because I cannot understand the contours of this reality if I am not constantly reminded that we are at the end of the century.

I search in the generation of Spanish literary luminaries closer to the Dominican intelligentsia, its sorrows and questionings, in order to see if they match my own and I find Pro Baroja and his proposal for a Republic of Intellectuals and I discard it, not because it was used to promote a dictatorship of the "intelligent ones," but because I imagine it a rather boring dictatorship and boredom is, among contemporary ailments, one of my own.

Some of the items proposed in the Manifest of 1901 of the so-called "Regenerationalists" (or The Generation of Disaster) of 1898, in Spain, written by Pro Baroja, Azorín, and Ramiro De Maeztu, seem to have been drafted for the Dominican Republic of our days.

I pour a cup of coffee and serve myself a papaya salad and I prepare for this moment of transcendental reflection, when the phone rings and a voice requests that I connect the fax. . . . The first assault of modernity, for which, happily, I had prepared by investing part of my meager savings in a machine that has blown off of the map for poets the need to wait for the mailman.

I turn the fax on automatic and I return to my reading of the Regenerationalists, or regenerated, and of some of their principles, which could be used as content in the present Dominican electoral campaign in order for us to avoid taking ourselves so seriously:

1. One of the typical traits of our time is the fast digestion of ideals. There is, in the moral ambience of this period in which we are living, an energetic ferment of discomposition, be it dogmas, utopias, metaphysical formulas. All that is not based on positivism and exactness, albeit born healthy and strong, is digested by the ambience with unbelievable speed.

Reproduced by permission from Adele S. Newson and Linda Strong-Leek, *Winds of Change: The Transforming of Caribbean Writers and Scholars* (New York: Peter Lang Publishing, Inc., 1998).

2. The Philosophers of our day, the most important ones, have tried to prove the relativity of absolute ideas.

3. We are witnessing the bankruptcy of dogmas; many of those that years ago appeared as beautiful utopias, today have been cracked, modified; they would accrue interests, they would serve to defend what has been created, but they lack the character of stability.

4. A wind of disquiet reigns in the world. Given the intellectual laxity of the country (it refers to Spain but it has its applications in its ex-colonies), given the national loss of a sense of morality, the most logical conclusion is to assume that the youth, following the steps of the majority of men of the previous generation, those fortunate ones will join political parties, and will live in the atmosphere of amorality of our public life; the failed ones will go on vituperating against country and governments from the forgotten corners of their offices or from the tables of a café.

The phone rings again. Yes? That I should please disconnect the fax so that I can receive a phone call? I run to disconnect the fax. . . .

"I regret to tell you that the university is not going to pay your hotel stay right away."

"Why is that?"

"Because that is the only way the State of Florida can protect itself against corruption."

"How is that? Does the University know that we are professional women writers (in saying this I take care to use my most severe of tones) and that in the past we have been invited by other institutions, some of them Ivy League schools! Those institutions paid us quite well and we did not even break a dish or a leaf in their property!"

"I am sorry. I really have nothing to do with this and if I charge your hotel to my credit card, I will not be reimbursed. Those are the laws of the State of Florida. But not to worry, we will refund your expenses by mail."

"How did you say we would be reimbursed?"

"By mail."

"Does the State of Florida realize that in this country mail tampering is not a federal crime?

"Does the State realize that in this city letters take more than six months to be delivered because our mailmen work on foot and do not visit streets where people don't write and they tend to accumulate the correspondence and to deliver it in large quantities twice a year?"

"You must be kidding."

"Kidding? This, my friend, is the Caribbean where a woman is trying to write, but I know, this has nothing to do with you."

I return to the Regenerationalists (by now sharing their pessimism):

5. Can one believe that the strength of all these useless people [they refer to the youth], without purpose, has nothing of value?

6. Can one believe it possible to love a country like that?

7. No, we ought not love a country for what it is, because it would continue to be thus eternally. But what it is ought not to move us not to love
it. To love the country as it is would be horrible; not to love it the way it
is would be horrendous. We need to love it ARBITRARILY, like (finally
we women show up in these reflections) mothers love their children
and like women love men. We must love it with a transcendental love.
                                   Manifiesto Regeneracionista, Spain, 1901

The recipient of such capacity for transcendental love, which I imagine
must also include the love for writing, or this craft so poorly appreciated,
I begin to recover my spiritual strength when I receive another fax. This time
it is sent by the travel agency.

"We need your credit card number in order to be able to make reservations in the hotel and to make sure you pay one day in advance, before your
arrival."

Hell! Now, besides assuming we Caribbean female writers are North American, they are assigning us a class status. A credit card? Where can a woman
writer today dig out, in these islands where college teaching is paid at a rate equivalent to four dollars an hour, five thousand dollars to deposit to get a credit card
to charge dollars, without having to pay a high rate of monthly interest?

"Do the Cuban women have a credit card?"

"No, and they will not be able to come."

I return to pour myself another cup of coffee and to reaffirm my pledge of
transcendental love for the craft of writing in order not to send the university
and the State of Florida to hell, and I rush to write about the topic that has
been assigned to me for my presentation, thinking that brilliant ideas are
worthless if the women writers who are to get together don't understand
the way we live and the conditions under which we labor, those of us trying
to write in these lairs. Without a fax, without a credit card, without dollars,
and generally without electricity. In Santo Domingo we experience fifteen to
twenty hours black-outs, because the solar lighting system that can be pur-
chased in Miami costs ten thousand dollars here, and the small converter we
have is not capable of accumulating sufficient voltage to ensure us at least
three hours of light to sit under to read or to write.

What is the challenge to the woman writer of today in islands such as
ours? Some fundamental theorists such as Edouard Glissant have already
posed the question in a much more lucid manner, and the poet Derek Walcott, awarded the Nobel Prize for Literature in 1992, has summarized this in
three verses:

I have Dutch, nigger and English in me,
and either I'm nobody
or I am a nation.
                  Derek Walcott, *The Schooner Flight: 1-Adios, Carenage*

And, if we were to think of ourselves as a nation, beyond the specific issues related to gender that frame us, which would be some of the essential

challenges before us? Edouard Glissant has formulated eight propositions for reflection for writers of the Caribbean which I offer for discussion:

1. *The Conflict between Similarities and Diversity.* Cultural similarities or "sameness," in this context, means the encompassing cultural world which the West imposed on our fragmented diversity. The weight of this similarity tends to interrupt the efforts of the human spirit to transcend a "universal" humanism which tries to assimilate all our national peculiarities. And, I add, there would be nothing wrong in it if it were not for the fact that *definitions of that* UNIVERSAL HUMANISM WERE ALSO GIVEN TO US BY THE WEST. Which are our own definitions? To answer this question represents the first conceptual challenge for Caribbean women and men authors.

2. *The Construction of Diversity.* A diversity that is not synonymous with sterility and chaos but is the creation of cross cultural relationships by individuals searching for an answer. Not by persons who are absorbed or swallowed by the predominant notion of culture, but by individuals who intend to create new relationships. Cultural similarity or "sameness" demands "imitators," "supervisors," and "disseminators." Diversity establishes BECOMING, OR TO ARRIVE AT BEING, as a fundamental principle. Is our creation a search for becoming or a search to succeed? To succeed as what?

3. *To Confront Creatively the Transition from the Written to the Oral.* The written is understood here as the result of the universal influence or the "sameness" and the oral as the ORGANIZED MANIFESTATION OF DIVERSITY. It seems, Glissant says, that the written acquires, each time and with more frequency, the role of ARCHIVE, and it is reserved for the very few. How are we dealing with the challenge to FEED THE ORAL INTO THE WRITTEN TEXT? The dream of Mallarmé of the universe becoming a book falls to pieces before the creative fragmentation of the Caribbean.

4. *The Creation of a National Literature.* I know that when I mention the word "national" (living in an island that is open and in a world practically without frontiers) some would think I do so in the old sense of ethnocentrism, chauvinism, or insular neurosis. To me, to make a national literature is to create a space for the emergence of new voices and new people, precisely those individuals left out by cultural similarity or "sameness." It means expressing that which characterizes us, that is to say, a system of relationships, under the aegis of diversity, without falling into regionalism, or into folklorisms that reflect only what a culture has been or was.

5. *To Understand That a National Language Is the Language Produced by the People of a Given Culture.* This means understanding that a national literature emerges when a community "whose collective existence is threatened" tries to define the reasons for its existence. If cultural alienation has an impact on the structure of literary creativity, should not the writing or the literature that seeks to express national idiosyncrasies be attached to the SEARCH FOR AN IDENTITY WHICH IS ALSO THE EXPRESSION OF THE DIVERSITY that frames us?

6. *To Begin to Define What Really Defines Us and the Techniques or Forms of Expression Which Ought to Express It.* I espouse the same questions as Glissant when he demands: Is the sonnet, with ends that both summarize and transcend

the meaning of the poem, a form for the expression of orality, for the apparent synchrony of the songs of the black population? Is the novel, conceived as an individual act, "set aside from the poetics of the group," a means in societies where the community plays a central role in the artistic production of its inhabitants? What are the genres we could call our own? What is the feminine specification in that "own"?

7. *The Creation of a Cross-Cultural Poetics and of a Sense of Caribbeanism.* I also espouse the reasoning of Glissant and Derek Walcott when they affirm: Our place is the Caribbean, and although our first stubborn reaction against the generalized universality is to remain where we are, our intellectual challenge is to create and to define a notion of Caribbeanism. Caribbeanism is a dream that frees us from the unilateral alternatives of a nationalism impossible in such small islands as ours and at the same time introduces us to a cross cultural process that modifies a stricken nationalism without undermining it. What are we really, Glissant asks us, but a series of multiple relationships and interrelationships, an opening that paradoxically encompasses us and defines us? Is this "we" the same for men and women of the Caribbean?

8. *To Express in a Participatory Manner the Dialectic of What Is from Within and from Without.* The expression of the dialectic between what is within and what is without, WITH THE PEOPLE AND FROM THE PEOPLE: their orality, their music, their painting, their sculpture, their dreams, their sorrows, is our greatest challenge and a topic of much discussion in literary conferences today on the role of women and men writers in the contemporary Caribbean.

The other challenges and problems to the women writers of today, those related to physical survival, social uncertainty such as "class," the difficulties in disseminating our work, the pros and cons of professionalization, the absence of a feminine and feminist criticism of our work that would project in all its dimensions our writing, are the same old problems that have had an impact on our lives since writing began, and although fundamental they are equivalent (in their challenge to our craft) to those related to the creation of a culture: a national culture that would mean the LOVING integration, the transcendental love we women are supposed to embody, of all of the voices we are today.

Attempting Perfection: An Interview with Judith Ortiz Cofer

Renee H. Shea

Judith Ortiz Cofer remembers that even as a young child in Puerto Rico, she knew instinctively that storytelling was a form of empowerment and that her *abuela* and the other women in her family told stories as a way of passing on power from one generation to another. Once she was educated, Cofer has said, she transferred that oral tradition into literature. In her poems, essays, novels, and short fiction, she tells stories of her Navy father whose "homecomings were the verses / we composed over the years making up / the siren's song that kept him coming back" ("My Father in the Navy," *Reaching for the Mainland* 25). In "Siempre," she recalls her mother, "still vibrant with her other selves," as

> the timidly exultant teenage bride, the anxiety-driven
> young mother in a strange country, and always
> the battle to keep loving life in spite of exile,
> loneliness [. . .]. (*A Love Story Beginning in Spanish* 19)

Cofer wonders about the term "macho man"—which she points out actually means "male man"—and reflects on the possibility of a woman having or being macho ("Taking the Macho," *Woman in Front of the Sun* 63–72). She writes about being an immigrant and muses whether we might all be immigrants in these days when we live in such a diverse cultural garden.

Born in Hormigueros, Puerto Rico and raised in the United States, primarily in New Jersey, Cofer is currently the Franklin Professor of English and Creative Writing at the University of Georgia. Her latest work is a collection of poetry, *A Love Story Beginning in Spanish*, published by the University of Georgia Press in 2005. In 2004, she published *Call Me Maria*, and in the previous year a novel, *The Meaning of Consuelo*, which was one of two winners of the 2003 Americas Award for Children's and Young Adult Literature. *Woman in Front of the Sun* (2000), written in prose and poetry, is her memoir about becoming a writer. Her novel *The Line of the Sun* (1989) was nominated for a Pulitzer Prize in 1989; *Silent Dancing: A Partial Remembrance of a Puerto Rican Childhood* (1990), a series of essays and poems, was awarded a Pen/Martha Alband Special Citation in Non-fiction; *The Latin Deli* (1995), also a collection of essays, short fiction and poetry, received the Anisfield Wolf Award for Race Relations in 1994; and The American Library Association named her collection of short stories, *An Island Like You: Stories of the Barrio* (1995), a Best Book of the Year for 1995–96.

Cofer is widely anthologized in textbooks for middle school, high school, and college and has contributed to magazines both literary and popular. She has won fellowships from the National Endowment for the Arts, the Witter Bynner Foundation for Poetry, the Rockefeller Foundation, and the Bread Loaf Writers' Conference.

Readers look to Cofer for her honest explorations into what it means to be bilingual and bicultural, to grow up, as she says, "with conflictive expectations: the pressures from my father to become very well versed in the English language and the Anglo customs, and from my mother not to forget where we came from" (Acost-Belen 93). She writes primarily in English, but says she "writes obsessively" about her Puerto Rican experience. She calls English her "literary language, the language [she] learned in the schools," and Spanish her "familial language" ("And Are You a Latina Writer?" *Woman in Front of the Sun* 105–115). In her poem "El Azul," she writes, "We dream in the language we all understand / in the tongue that preceded alphabet and word" (*Woman in Front of the Sun* 126).

Cofer can be playful about her heritage in such poems as "Latin Women Pray" where she imagines "Margarita, Josefina, Maria, and Isabel / All fervently hoping that if not omnipotent," God might "at least be bilingual" (*Reaching for the Mainland* 27). Her appeal, however, draws readers with concerns unlimited by category and classification. In "Don't Misread My Signals," an often anthologized essay, she writes about the stereotyping of Latina women, and "In Search of My Mentors' Gardens," she muses on Alice Walker's warning not to be content with "segregated literature" (*Woman in Front of the Sun* 91–104). She is inspired by a wide range of writers, including Virginia Woolf, Flannery O'Connor, and Walker herself, as well as the Spanish-language writers Miguel Cervantes, Pablo Neruda, and Isabel Allende.

Renee Shea interviewed Judith Ortiz Cofer on 21 April 2005.

RS: How did you choose the provocative title *A Love Story Beginning in Spanish* for your new book? Why did you decide to put together this collection of poems, many of which you published before in journals and magazines?

JC: Poetry books are usually formed that way. You publish a lot of different poems in journals and at some point you feel that you have a critical mass. The poems in this collection date back as far as fourteen years, so it's a new book in that it's newly collected work. I've always felt that a poetry book has to coalesce, come together in form, so I don't write poetry in the same way I write novels, which is with one idea in mind. I have quite a few poems that I kept looking at and wondering if they made a book, and about two or three years ago I thought a pattern was emerging—not just a thematic pattern but a way of looking at the book as a whole. I thought that at this point in my life when I'm 53 years old and have lived most of my life in the United States but never left my connection to the island behind, there was finally a story in my poetry; and it had to do with coming from Spanish, beginning in Spanish on the island where I was born and my parents were married, to my present situation, which is that I live in Georgia. I consider this my home. I have a family and a love story here.

I think all human life is a love story—not necessarily a romantic story but one of connections you make along the way. Mine began in Spanish and is now in English, but it goes back to Spanish. What I wanted was for the poems to reflect that, to have a sense of continuation. So that's where the idea came from. The love story has to do with the fact that I have a very strong narrative impulse. Even when I'm writing poetry, I'm thinking in terms of how this affects my narrative, how I can plug it into a narrative. I don't think in manipulative terms, but that's how my brain works. I had originally thought that the title poem, "El Amor: A Story Beginning in Spanish" would be the first, but I thought in a way that announces that the story has closure, so I moved it to the end because that poem says a story can begin anywhere in any language at any time. I wanted it to remain open to indicate that the story is always happening. It's an *Ars Poetica*.

RS: When you republish a poem as part of a book do you revise it? Do you feel that's cricket? Or is the poem frozen in the moment in time when you first published it?

JC: Absolutely, I revise. The poem is mine and it belongs to the journal only when it first appears. I think it was Auden who said a poem is never really finished; we just abandon it at some point. To me, poetry is an attempt at the perfection of language, which is, of course, impossible in human terms. But every time I look at a line, I ask myself, "Can it be made better?" Coleridge said a good poem is "the best words in the best order." That sounds simple, but what is best? Many of the poems that are now in this book appear from slightly changed to dramatically changed because *I* have changed and learned a few things.

RS: There are several Penelope poems in the section "From a Sailor's Wife's Journal." How did they come about?

JC: The actual genesis of those and some on the Bible as well came from my having to teach both parts of a world literature course when I was first starting out. I had to read these texts very carefully, and I started feeling cheated out of the voice of Penelope. I thought her story was more interesting than Odysseus's. His was episodic: then I did this; then I had an affair with Calypso, which is all very fascinating. But Penelope's personal life interested me.

I was also interested because Penelope was a sailor's wife, as was my mother. I don't think people need to know that as any woman will recognize Penelope's anguish and her need to fly off and have a life outside of the palace. I started a series of these poems, and the ones in the book are only a small portion because I found myself weaving and unweaving, as Penelope was doing, trying to get her out of the house.

RS: They seem more romantic than many I've read (such as Carol Ann Duffy's "Penelope") which are more feminist talking-back readings. Yours seem dreamy almost—a saddened Penelope, but one still longing for her beloved Odysseus.

JC: I don't see them as romantic. I see the first poem, "Dear Odysseus," as a woman in love yearning to go with her man and for her man to return. But I see the series as a progressive separation. She remembers him as this romantic hero who doesn't want to stay on the farm. She also sees the carolers and partiers coming home from a pagan ritual and having made love and drunk wine, and there's a yearning there. So I saw Penelope's separation not as, "Oh I'm liberated now; I think I'll raise hell," but as an intellectual and emotional coming to terms with her independence. So the poems are meditative in that way. I see my Penelope coming to liberation but not getting up on a stage and announcing, "I'm a liberated woman now." That's not how it happened to my mother or a lot of women. First it's emotional. I tried to infuse those poems with images of flight and the freedom that she's considering.

RS: Your Penelope is also very attuned to her own sexuality.

JC: That reflects my kind of feminism, which doesn't reject the romance of the flesh, doesn't reject a woman admitting that she's weak in love but strong in her mind. Maybe that's my Latina-ness, but I've never felt the need to grandstand my liberation. It's internal, and I try to live life as a free woman. But that doesn't eliminate the possibility of being connected to another human being through passion and sexuality.

RS: For some time, I've wanted to ask you about the hibiscus. Obviously, this flower means a great deal to you (it's a hallmark of your website). What's your connection to this "ephemeral" flower?

JC: You're getting the inside story in a way. This was a gift I made for my daughter. The poem was originally dedicated to Tanya. The hibiscus represents my background. It was the first flower I became aware of as a child because it was all over the island. In *Silent Dancing*, I talk about how the hibiscus was everywhere. As little girls, my cousins and I used to play with them. We rolled them up and pretended they were cigarettes; we put them in our hair; they represented the island. But in this poem, there's the one thing I didn't think about as a child: how brief the life of the hibiscus is, how beautiful it is in full bloom, and how suddenly it wraps itself into a little shroud. It allowed me a moment of meditation about a woman's beauty in her life.

The reader doesn't need to know this, but this was a time when my daughter—who is a mathematician and a wonderful gardener and cook (unlike her mother)—was feeling depressed. I took her this hibiscus that I had bought and, before I gave it to her, I looked up information about it. That description yielded the images in the poem. It's a sort of *carpe diem* poem—not an original theme, but it says to enjoy the flower, understand it is beautiful and also has practical uses, and that it can suddenly disappear. It is short-lived.

RS: This collection opens with a quote from Denise Levertov: "You invaded my country by accident, / not knowing you had crossed the border." Is she one of your favorites?

JC: When I was an undergraduate in college, she was one of the few female poets I found in anthologies. She wrote about the Vietnam War, but I thought that the line—"you invaded my country"—could be taken in any number of ways. I wanted an ironic reversal on immigration: I have not invaded your country; this culture has invaded my country and my internal country, too. I found her words particularly appropriate for what I was trying to do.

RS: I want to turn to *Call Me Maria* now. In your letter to the reader that you did for the publisher, you quote [Constantine] Cavafy's poem "Ithaka"—more Homer. You seem to have a real connection to *The Odyssey*.

JC: I can't help but be an English teacher, and this seminal story of loss, separation, and beauty mirrors everything I have known in my life: my father was a veteran of every war since Korea until he died and my mother lived a life of exile and waiting. We were influenced by history because my father was always involved in it. We were brought to the US but lived in a bubble of culture. *The Odyssey* has been key to understanding the recurrent nature of certain events. In this ancient text, Homer brought in the idea of the family waiting for the warrior, and it gave me a framework for thinking about my life. In fact, I recently wrote a chapter for a high school textbook on Cavafy because I love his work. Those lines, "As you set out for Ithaka / hope the voyage is a long one, / full of adventure, full of discovery," have meant a lot to me because my father's journey was long and full of adventure but not happy, and I wanted something different for me and my child.

RS: This book crosses multiple genres with its poetry, narratives, and letters; indeed, you call it "a novel in letters, poems, and prose." How does something like that start with a poem? When did you know this "novel" would be multi-genre?

JC: When I started thinking about this book, I was doing a lot of traveling and trying to keep a notebook and I asked myself, "Who is the character?" I often do this. In order to think about a character or a situation, I will start a poem about it. To me, poetry is a door to a place that may be lost in my brain. When I am writing a poem, I actually have to set an alarm—and this is not mystical, it's psychological—because I enter a place where I am trying to do what psychologists do in deep analysis. Some of the poems toward the end of the book came to me first, and that's how I started entering Maria's brain or personality.

At some point, I had all these pieces, which I sent to my editor and said, "I think I'm going to try writing this book in sections because this is how it's coming to me." She liked some of the pieces so much that I started thinking of Maria as someone watching the world, collecting and trying to make a collage of some sort appear. As soon as I knew she lived in a basement apartment and was watching the world go by through the top half of her window and that she heard voices and was separated from the world, I started thinking in terms of what impressions she was gathering. So I had her writing things about her teachers, about her friends, the smell of cologne. She comforts herself in her initial loneliness by trying to construct the world. The more I wrote and sent to my editor, the more she liked the idea of allowing Maria's voice to emerge.

RS: So much of your work is about writing, literally and figuratively writing oneself into the world. But this one has an even stronger emphasis on language. Again, I am quoting your letter to your reader: "I wanted Maria to learn to give meaning to her journey by becoming a recorder of experience, that is, a writer." Can you talk a little about why you did that? Because it seems to me that making her so specifically a writer might narrow the audience that feels connected to her.

JC: I hope that hasn't happened. When I go to schools, often with immigrant students, the last thing they think about is the writer. What they see is that she is a girl desperately trying to find a place and to find language. She just happens to use writing. They mainly talk about her relationships with Whoopi and Uma, her *abuela*, her parents. The fact that she is a writer is coincidental to many of these kids. They seem to think of the writing as a way she has found to integrate herself into the *barrio*.

RS: As you were writing those poems that are about grammar and syntax, the technical elements of language as in "English Declaration: I Am the Subject of the Sentence" or "English: I am the Simple Sentence" did you have in mind a kind of a didactic purpose for your young audience?

JC: Not at all. I'm completely against didacticism in art. I think any lessons in art should be subliminal and playful. I thought of this as simply a frame for where the kids go during the day. They have to put up with teachers telling them about grammar and sentences. I tried to imagine myself, and I was nerdish, so Maria takes these boring exercises she was given to do and makes them into poems.

RS: I have to say that this one is a Valentine to teachers, most of all to your husband, I think (though he's a math teacher).

JC: The whole book is dedicated to my husband. The students call him Mr. C. He teaches math, and I wrote that poem "Math Class: Sharing the Pie" completely about him. Talk about an idealist! People think that because I'm the poet that I'm the idealist, but it's not true. My husband teaches for almost no money in a school that sees a lot of poverty in rural Georgia. He spends 10- or 12-hour days trying to convince kids math is beautiful. One thing I did that was kind of strange was that I imagined my husband in a school in New York but yearning for Georgia. I wanted Maria to see that her nostalgia and loneliness was not just because she was a Puerto Rican girl, but that there could be this white guy from the South also yearning for a completely different landscape and also feeling alienated and lost. Mr. Golden is a poet who tells the kids he has learned math by counting birds, so this is a tribute to the heroes of the classroom, the ones who really do care.

RS: Maria has to be one of your favorite characters. You've made her into such an exceptional person. Is she?

JC: I like her because even though she is a bookworm, she is completely involved in life. Maria and I are only similar in a few ways: her parents are not mine, but what I like about her is that she chooses to be with the parent who needs her the most. She doesn't choose the easy life, but she loves her father despite the fact that he's a mess. She despairs at his womanizing and drinking, but she is still his collaborator. I like her not so much because she's a bookworm like me, but because she jumps into life and doesn't take the easy way out.

RS: Comparisons to *House on Mango Street* by Sandra Cisneros seem inevitable. Were you inspired by Esperanza and her quest? Or do you see these more as parallel tracks?

JC: I considered that, but I think *Maria* is different. The form [of vignettes, poetry and prose] may be similar, but I've done this before in *The Latin Deli*. Sandra did a fabulous job and no one can imitate *The House on Mango Street*. But I knew the comparisons would be made because we're both Latina. Still, I don't think Esperanza and Maria are the same. Do you?

RS: Both are writers. Both seem to be finding an individual voice to speak for the community.

JC: But Maria stays. She's not just interested in telling the stories. She wants to find a voice for herself. Esperanza is gaining power so she can leave and tell the stories, but Maria chooses to stay in the *barrio*. But any comparison to Sandra I consider a great compliment.

RS: Also, in that letter to the "reader" you wrote, "Language wins you friendship and buys you freedom." I doubt that Spanish or Spanglish always wins you friends. Doesn't it marginalize some readers?

JC: This may sound harsh, but I am not thinking of the reader when I'm writing; I'm thinking of the story. If it requires Spanish or Spanglish, that's what I put in, mainly because I think of reading literary works as work, not simply entertainment. When I was trying to become an English teacher and find an identity for myself, I read everything I was told to read. The greatest works often contain many other languages: Greek in *The Waste Land* [by T.S. Eliot], Italian with [Ezra] Pound, French with many people. I just assumed if I couldn't grasp the meaning in context, if the work was important enough and we were interested enough, that we would go find a dictionary and look things up. So, in order to create the world that Maria lives in, I could not write all standard English. I try to use my art and craft to provide context, but I expect my reader to find a way to understand the culture I'm writing about.

RS: In another interview, you said that you're not a political writer "in that [you] never take an issue and write a story about it [. . .] the politics are background noise" (Acosta-Belen 85). Yet the stand you implicitly take about language seems very political.

JC: Is nobody going to read Mark Twain because of the dialect? Or Zora Neale Hurston? I claim the right as a writer to have my characters speak credibly in their chosen form. I may not be a political writer, but it doesn't mean I'm not a political person. My politics are infused in my work.

RS: Politics are certainly infused in *The Meaning of Consuelo*, and I wonder if Consuelo is a character you couldn't have written until now. Is she someone you wouldn't have been able to get inside of even, say, ten years ago?

JC: That's very insightful. In many of the reviews, Consuelo is called "grim" or kind of dark. But this is a story I had to write when I felt I had enough distance from and compassion for my culture. I love all the celebratory aspects of the Puerto Rican culture and I feel so grateful to have come from a culture that has yielded so much for my work. But there are also things that bother me, such as the homophobia and how the Catholic Church has conspired to maintain this sense of the woman as servant, the suffering one. In this book, I wanted a girl growing up during a time when she saw options and had to make painful choices to define herself.

That's why I called it *The Meaning of Consuelo*. Consuelo means "comfort." She was born and raised to play a part and at some point she has to define what Consuelo means and decide that she will be her own Consuelo, her own comfort. I had to know something first. That takes living. It could not have been my first novel.

RS: This is your first real mainstream press book. It's published by Farrar, Strauss & Giroux. Has this made a big difference? I know you've talked about appreciating the support of smaller presses yet feeling frustrated by the lack of resources for both ensuring a first-rate presentation and promoting the book. Is this a breakthrough? Why do you think FSG was interested in it? Was it because of your reputation and prizes or the story itself?

JC: I haven't moved into the mainstream. I'm not a bestselling author in terms of huge numbers. My great luck is that my work is used extensively in high school and college textbooks. I think Farrar, Strauss & Giroux took a chance on me. I've been very aware that I have a public, but it doesn't have to do with the masses—just a faithful, loyal following.

There's not a linear progression of success as though I started out with a little press and worked up to FSG. I am thrilled to be published with them, and Beacon Press has done a fabulous job with the paperback. But every book is different. Recently, University of Georgia Press did something very courageous. They commissioned a translation of *Woman in Front of the Sun*, and it's coming out in Spanish (*Mujer Frente al Sol*). Poetry is almost impossible to place. University of Georgia Press has been loyal and has kept my books in print no matter what the numbers, so I give them the poetry. If I write another novel, my agent will send it around, and it will find a publisher.

RS: You've written about your grandmother's influence on you through her storytelling and much more (though she was not formally educated). You pointed out in an interview with Stephanie Gordon that she belonged to a generation of women who did not need "political rhetoric" in order to establish themselves as "liberated women." What exactly did you mean?

JC: I think that part of my stance as a feminist comes from my grandmother as well as my mother. Mama (my name for her; Mami is my mother) never doubted her own power for one minute; yet she was maternal, nurturing, and as feminine as any woman I've ever known. She did not feel that one negated the other. She empowered herself internally. She didn't have to go around saying, "I am woman, hear me roar"; she just roared! She was a great model because she took action. She was a great problem solver, and yet she never talked about her philosophy of feminism. I just knew that all of her actions were based on her ethical system. I watched her be powerful without giving up the things she wanted to have. I've said that I knew I wanted my art but I didn't want to give up being a wife and mother to have it. So many women of my generation at some point in their lives came to believe that it was not possible to have a family and be liberated as a feminist. That was an early way of looking at things. If someone asked my grandmother who wears the pants in the family, she'd say, "Well, your grandfather does, but why would I need to wear pants? I have the power."

RS: When asked where you see literature going in the US in the next two decades in your interview with Lorraine Lopez, you predicted that a new generation of people from diverse cultural backgrounds, and who have gone through the education system, will be creating a literature that represents the true diversity of this country. I think about your grandmother here, but aren't you also describing Maria and Consuelo?

JC: Isn't that funny? It takes you to tell me what I think! When I created Maria and Consuelo, I was thinking not of myself, but, particularly with Maria, I was thinking of someone who embraces a multitude of tongues and who chooses to speak standard English when it is necessary in the same way African-Americans speak one dialect in the home but understand that when they're on Wall Street they speak the language of the mainstream. So, right now in my honors undergraduate writing class, I have a girl from Egypt and another from Greece. They're writing stories about leaving their countries and coming to Atlanta, and I think how wonderful if one of these girls becomes a writer—a Southern writer.

RS: When I saw you last October, you commented that your students are your "daily news" and that without this interaction you would live your life more and more internally. Could you talk about that? Could it possibly be true that gregarious as you are, you are, in fact, more inclined toward being an introvert than an extrovert?

JC: Actually, yes. Being gregarious is my public persona. When I am not traveling or teaching, I'm usually very alone in what my husband calls "the cave" or "the dungeon." I keep the drapes drawn and everything quiet. I have always had a need for solitude because I live in my mind. I love a day when I don't have to do what I do today: meet students, go to a meeting, a dinner. I will enjoy every minute of these activities because that is how I absorb life. But then tomorrow I will enjoy staying in my pajamas and working alone in my basement with only one light on. I'm afraid if I didn't have these requirements of students waiting for me, I would more and more live in my mind because that's where my imagination resides. I understand the need for both, which is why I choose to have a family and to teach.

RS: I've heard you say many times that you carved out writing time for yourself by reserving 5 to 7 A.M. each day, starting when you had a young daughter. Do you still do that? Do you write every day?

JC: I still do mainly because I've trained myself. People who run or do one thing obsessively or compulsively at a certain hour find that it becomes a need. I find that my best work comes when I have not spoken to anyone yet; when I've just been asleep the whole night before I can easily move into this realm right from dreams. It doesn't always end at 7 A.M. now because I have more leisure, but I find that about three hours is all I can do.

RS: I love seeing the eclecticism of your influences just by reading the epigraphs and introductions to your books: Pablo Neruda, Denise Levertov, Virginia Woolf, May Sarton, W. S. Mervin—across time and culture. You must be a voracious reader.

JC: Out of need and pleasure. One of the things I've been doing lately is taking the writers that I love and reading them from beginning to end.

I did that with Flannery O'Connor last summer: all letters, stories, books. I just got everything of [Vladimir] Nabokov to read, but I haven't started yet. But the other thing is that I am on endless comprehensive exam committees. Writers are not like scholars because they put together weird lists of what they want to be examined on. I just finished one that made me reread Aristotle's *Poetics*! I may have read these things a long time ago, but once again my students keep me reading far and wide.

RS: But other influences are Alice Walker and Flannery O'Connor; and you know that one of my very favorite pieces of yours is "In Search of My Mentors' Gardens" where you talk about them. It seems that you're able to take in so many different approaches and influences, even styles, and appreciate them for being one thing or another without judging them.

JC: This is the thing I tell my graduate students. Everybody feels that they have to write out their own experience and feelings, but the master works of literature were written when the writers entered another consciousness—even that of a giant cockroach! I tell them, if you're an African-American and reading only African-American writers, all you are seeing are things you need to know for yourself as a human being but not as an artist. An artist has to take in *everything*. One of the things I do when I'm teaching a poetry seminar is have my poor graduate assistants go to the library and find every poetry anthology from every poetry ghetto—like Lesbian Poetry Writers of the 1950s or Puerto Ricans Angry at the World along with the Norton Anthology and others—and tell them they must read at least one book per week *out of themselves*. I say, "Does it matter if that poem gives you chills? Does it matter that this poet is a white guy in Vermont?" One of the things I believe in—and maybe I'm sounding political now, but I am a dictator in class—is that people have been taught that they can only think in terms of themselves and write in those terms. That is so wrong. I have found the greatest artistic lessons from people whose lives I think are reprehensible. I dislike the way James Dickey lived his life, especially the way he treated women, but I still cry when I read some of his poems, so one has to separate the personal from art. And I have to practice what I preach. So, I read people on my students' reading lists whom I wouldn't normally turn to, and often I learn even more about myself.

RS: Virginia Woolf certainly isn't inimical to your belief system, though she lived a very different life and came from a different background and time. Yet, you've written about what a profound influence she's had on you.

JC: Models are a gift, but you have to discover what you need; and with her, I found an intelligent woman's voice saying, "Dig in your own backyard. You have treasures. Go back into your memory. Follow the track left by some emotions to your 'moments of being.'"

RS: I want to follow up on a wonderful point you made in your interview with Lorraine Lopez when you talked about reading and writing being separate activities (you were explaining why you would not choose to read aloud certain of your works). You referred to "the eloquent silence" between the writer and the reader. What is that "eloquent silence"?

JC: When I'm reading a story in complete solitude, there is this voice in my head implanting invaluable lessons, so there's a silence in a mystical yet biologically understandable way passing information from an object in your hand into your most important condition as a human being, your unconscious mind. So the "eloquent silence" is between the text, writer, and reader, even if the writer wrote hundreds of years ago. Reading is probably the most important thing I do for myself.

RS: I read somewhere that you're working on a novel with an old woman as the protagonist?

JC: I never finished that. I started a novel some time ago about an old woman who used to be a dancer and was in Miami. But I realized I didn't know enough about this woman. I still think about her. Perhaps some day. I've written so much in the voice of a young person that I definitely want to turn that around.

RS: What are you working on now?

JC: Because I just finished three books in two years and collaborated on this translation, I'm now just planning. I have about 50 pages of notes toward a novel, but don't want to talk about it because I don't know if it will happen.

RS: But you're always writing poetry, what you've called "the ultimate discipline"?

JC: I work on poems all the time. I have several new ones, but they're not ready to send out. I'm in the gathering stage right now with notes all over my table.

WORKS CITED

Acosta-Belén, Edna. "An Interview with Judith Ortiz Cofer." *MELUS* (Fall 1993): 84–99.

Gordon, Stephanie. "An Interview with Judith Ortiz Cofer." *AWP Chronicle* (October/November 1997): 1–9.

López, Lorraine. "Possibilities for Salsa Music in the Mainstream: An Interview with Judith Ortiz Cofer." http://www.english.uga.edu/~jcofer/vita.html.

Ortiz Cofer, Judith. *A Love Story Beginning in Spanish; Poems.* Athens, Georgia: University of Georgia Press, 2005.

———. *Call Me María.* New York: Scholastic, 2004.

———. *The Meaning of Consuelo.* New York: Farrar, Strauss & Giroux, 2003.

———. *Woman in Front of the Sun: On Becoming A Writer.* Athens, Georgia: University of Georgia Press, 2000.

————. *An Island Like You: Stories of the Barrio.* New York: Penguin, 1995.

————. *Reaching for the Mainland and Selected New Poems.* Tempe: Bilingual Press Review, 1995.

————. *The Latin Deli.* Athens, GA & London: University of Georgia Press, 1993.

————. *Silent Dancing: A Partial Remembrance of a Puerto Rican Childhood.* University of Houston: Arte Publico Press, 1990.

————. *The Line of the Sun.* Athens, Georgia: University of Georgia Press, 1989.

I Write These Messages That Come

María Irene Fornés

Thoughts come to my mind at any point, anywhere—I could be on the subway—and if I am alert enough and I have a pencil and paper, I write these *messages* that come. It might be just a thought, like a statement about something, an insight, or it could be a line of dialogue. It could be something that someone says in my head.

I have a box filled with these scribbles. Some of them are on paper napkins or the backs of envelopes. These things are often the beginning of a play. Most of the lyrics of the songs that I write are based on these notes—as opposed to a play, which, once it starts, *I* make. I usually gather a number of those things that have some relation—again, I do not even know why I consider that they are related—and I put them together. I compose something around those messages using a number of lines that have come into my head.

Now sometimes I am trying to get myself organized, and I am sharpening pencils and doing all those things. So I go to that pile of notes—it's a mess because it is scribblings. Sometimes I cannot read what I wrote because often I make notes in dark theaters when I am sitting through a play. (A lot of thoughts come into my mind when I am watching a play, especially a play that I am not at all absorbed by.) I start typing through some of these things and very often I find things I cannot imagine why in the world I thought they were anything special. They are the most mundane thoughts or phrases. Sometimes I think, "There is some value here that I do not recognize now, but at *some* point I thought, 'This is a message.' It must be that it is, but I have lost the thought." When that happens I often type it out and leave it, even though it is without any faith at all. I leave it because at some point I did have this faith.

The feeling I have about these messages is very different from what I have about what I am writing when it is *I* writing. I might write something that

María Irene Fornés, "'I Write These Messages That Come,'" transcribed and edited by Robb Creese. *TDR: The Drama Review* VOLUME 21, NUMBER 4, ISSUE T76, December, 1977, 25–40.

I like, and it feels good. But the feeling I have about those other things is really as if it is a message that comes in an indivisible unit. I feel if a word is changed, then it is lost. A thought comes—sometimes I do not have a pencil with me—I try to repeat it in my head until I get to a pencil. I know I must remember the exact construction of the sentence. I might be wrong, you see. It could be that it does not matter more or less how it is said. But still I feel that it is a block and that is how it should look, whether it is a page of dialogue that comes in the message or three pages or one line.

That dialogue then could become a play. When I am to write a work, I never start from a blank page. I only start from one of these things that I do, that I receive. Sometimes I start a play from one line of dialogue. It has to be something that has the makings of a play.

The only play that I started from an idea—and it was an idea that was very clear in my head—and that I sat down and wrote was *Tango Palace.* I think it is quite clear that that is how it is written because the play has a very strong, central idea. None of my other plays does. They are not Idea Plays. My plays do not present a thesis, or at least, let us say, they do not present a formulated thesis. One can make a thesis about anything (I could or anyone could formulate one), but I do not present ideas except in *Tango Palace.* I lost interest in that way of working.

The play writes itself. The first draft writes itself anyway. Then I look at it and I find out what is in it. I find out where I have overextended it and what things need to be cut. I see where I have not found the scene. I see what I have to do for the character to exist fully. Then I rewrite. And of course in the rewrite there is a great deal of thought and sober analysis.

One day I was talking to Rochelle Owens, and I was telling her how when I start working on a play the words are just on paper. Perhaps I will see some things or I hear something. I feel the presence of a character or person. But then there is a point when the characters become crystallized. When that happens, I have an image in full color, technicolor. And that *happens!* I do not remember it happening, but I get it like *click!* At some point I see a picture of the set with the characters in it—let us say a picture *related* to the set, not necessarily the exact set.

The colors for me are very, very important. And the colors of the clothes the people wear. When it finally happens, the play exists; it has taken its own life. And then I just listen to it. I move along with it. I let it write itself. I have reached that point in plays at times. I have put scripts away then and picked them up three years later, and, reading them, suddenly I see that same picture with the same colors. The color never goes away. It could be ten years later. The play exists even if I have not finished writing it. Even if it is only fifteen pages. It is like an embryo that is already alive and it is there waiting.

I am always amazed how an audience knows when a play is finished. That is something that I have always found very beautiful. Sometimes when I go to the theater when it is not written in the program that there is going to be an intermission, and when it is quite clear that something has ended, people say, "Is it over?" But they say it with surprise. The actors have left the stage, but it does not look over. People know. And then when it is really over, there is that immediate knowledge that it has ended, and people applaud. In that same way, I know when a script has completed itself. I sense the last note of the play.

One play of mine has about three endings. It looks like it has ended, but then there is another ending, and then there is another ending. These are *almost-endings,* and they do not have that total satisfaction of a real ending. It could have been that I could have left it. But probably people would have been asking, "Is it over?" "Oh, it's over."

The characters: They talk. And when it talks, a character starts developing itself. I never try to reproduce a real character. I did, in fact, try to reproduce real people that I knew in one play, *The Office.* I got into trouble because the characters in the situation were from real life, and I changed a lot of things in the play. I felt that I lacked the objectivity to make the play really sharp and for me to be sure exactly what I was doing. Since I started with a reality of what happened, it was the event that was important. And that event would not work for the play.

I know a lot of people write either about a real person or else they put a familiar character into an invented situation. I find that it just confuses me, that I do not see that as useful for me in any way.

In that same conversation with Rochelle Owens, I told her about my colors. She found it very interesting. And I said, "You mean you don't see color when you write? I thought everybody saw color!" But she does not. I asked what happens to her, and she said she hears voices. She hears the sound of what the play is saying. Sometimes she is writing and she knows that a sentence should be bah-bah-bah-bah, but the words do not come immediately. Rather than stopping, she goes on and she leaves that blank space. She goes on because the other words are coming. She knows how it has to sound, and she goes back to it. It comes in exactly that form. That is very different from my own work.

Everything that I have written has had a different start. *Successful Life of 3* started when I heard two men speaking to each other. One of them was an actor I knew. That conversation was actually in my head. Not that I wanted to write the play for that actor, it is just that he was there and this other guy was there, and he did not have a very definite face. That caught my imagination completely. I wrote the play in two weeks.

At the same time, I was writing *Promenade,* which I wrote as an exercise I gave myself. I wrote down the characters on one set of index cards. On another set of cards, I wrote different places. I shuffled them together. I picked a card that said, "The Aristocrats." And I picked the card that said, "The Prison." So the play started in prison for that reason. But I found it very difficult to write a scene with aristocrats in prison, so the first thing that happened was that they were digging a hole to escape. I wanted to get them out of there.

For some reason it worked for me that the prisoners remained prisoners. And in the next scene, they were at a banquet where there were aristocrats. After that, I found using the cards for the characters was not helping me at all. But I kept using the place cards. That is why the play has six different locations. I would write a scene and when I was finished writing that scene I would turn to the next card. That was the order the scenes came in.

By the way, I find doing exercises very valuable. It is good for me not to do things too deliberately: to have half my mind on something else and *let* something start happening. I am really very analytical. I like analyzing things, but it is better for me not to think very much. Only after I have started creating can I put all my analytical mind into it. Most of my plays start with a kind of a fantasy game—just to see what happens. *Fefu and Her Friends* started that way. There was this woman I fantasized who was talking to some friends. She took her rifle and shot her husband. . . .

A playwright has a different distance from each script. Some are two feet away, and some are two hundred feet away. *Fefu* was not even two inches away. It is right where I am. That is difficult to do when one feels close. A different kind of delicacy enters into the writing. Each day I had to put myself into the mood to write the play. I wrote it in a very short period of time, in a very intense period of writing, where I did nothing but write, write, write. Every day I would start the day by reading my old folder (a different folder from the one where I keep my "messages"), where I have all my sufferings, personal sufferings: the times when I was in love and not, the times I did badly, all those anguishes which were really very profound. There were times that I just had to sit down and write about it because I felt anguish about it. It was not writing for the sake of writing; it was writing for the sake of exorcism. A lot of those things had been in this folder for many years. I had never looked at them. That was where the cockroaches were, so to speak.

I would start the day by reading something from that folder. Actually, there were even a couple times when I used things I found there, but most of it is garbage, really garbage, a collection of dirt: the whining, the complaining. But it would put me into that very, very personal, intimate mood to write.

I never before set up any kind of environment to write a play! This was the first time that I did that because the play was different. I had to reinforce the intimacy of the play.

Then I would put on the records of a Cuban singer, Olga Guillot. She is very passionate and sensuous. She is shameless in her passion. And I wrote the whole play listening to Olga Guillot. (My neighbors must have thought I was out of my mind.) There was one record, *Añorando el Caribe*, that particularly seemed to make my juices run. I just left it on the turntable and let it go on and on and on. The play had nothing to do with Olga Guillot. Her spirit is very different. She is very dramatic. And *Fefu* is very subtle and very delicate. But her voice kept me oiled.

I started the final writing of *Fefu* in February 1977. At that time I had about a third of the play written. It opened May 5, 1977. In those three months, I finished writing, I cast it, and I rehearsed it. I finished the play four days before it opened. I do not mean the very last scene. There were scenes in the middle I had to do. I made no revisions during rehearsals. I have to do some rewriting of the play now. I believe I must approach the rewrite in the same way as before: with the pile of writing and Olga Guillot.

Space affected *Fefu and Her Friends*. In late February, I decided to look for a place to perform the work. I had finished the first scene, and I had loose separate scenes that belonged somewhere in the second part of the play. I did not like the space I found because it had large columns. But then I was taken backstage to the rooms the audience could not see. I saw the dressing room, and I thought, "How nice. This could be a room in Fefu's house." Then I was taken to the greenroom. I thought that this also could be a room in Fefu's house. Then we went to the business office to discuss terms. That office was the study of Fefu's house. (For the performance we took some of the stuff out, but we used the books, the rugs, everything that was there.) I asked if we could use all of their rooms for the performances, and they agreed.

I had written Julia's speech in the bedroom already. I had intended to put it onstage, and I had not yet arrived at how it would come about. Part of the kitchen scene was written, but I had thought it would be happening in the living room. So I had parts of it already. It was the rooms themselves that modified the scenes which originally I planned to put in the living room.

People asked me, when the play opened, if I had written those scenes to be done in different rooms and then found the space. No. They were written that way because the space was there. I had to figure out the exact coordination for the movements between one scene and the other so the timing would be right. I had rehearsed each scene separately. Now I was going to rehearse them simultaneously. Then I realized that my play, *Aurora*, had exactly the same concept. There was the similarity of two different rooms with simultaneous life. I did not consciously realize until then that it had some connection with *Aurora*.

I mention this because people put so much emphasis on the deliberateness of a work. I am delighted when something is not deliberate. I do not trust deliberateness. When something happens by accident, I trust that the play is making its own point. I feel something is happening that is very profound and very important. People go far in this thing of awareness and deliberateness; they go further and further. They go to see a play and they do not like it. So someone explains it to them, and they like it better. How can they *possibly* understand it better, like it better, or see more of it because someone has explained it?

I am very good at explaining things. And whatever I do not understand, I can even invent. There are people who do beautiful work and do not know why, and they think it is invalid. Those who are not good at explanation are at a disadvantage, but their work is as valid.

I think it is impossible to aim at an audience when writing a play. I never do. I think that is why some commercial productions fail. They are trying to create a product that is going to create a reaction, and they cannot. If they could, every play on Broadway that is done for that purpose would be a great success. They think they know. They try and they fail. I know I do not know, but even if I did, I do not think I would write for the audience.

As a matter of fact, when the audience first comes to one of my plays, my feeling is that they are intruders. Especially when I have directed the play, I feel that I love my play so much, and I enjoy it so and feel so intimate with the actors, that when opening night arrives I ask, "What are all those people doing in my house?" Then it changes, of course, especially if they like it. I might even think I wrote it for them if they like it. I love to have an audience like a play.

But during the work period, they are never present. Basically I feel that if I like something, other people will like it, too.

I think there is always a *person* I am writing for. Sometimes it is a specific person that I feel is there with me enjoying it in my mind. In my mind, that person is saying, "Oh, yes, I love it!" Or if it is not a specific person, it is a kind of person. It might be someone who does not really have a face, but it is a friend, someone who likes the same things. If we saw a play, we both would like it or we both would dislike it. So in a way I am writing for an "audience." But it is not for the public, not for the critics, not the business of theater.

I feel that the state of creativity is a very special state. And most people who write or who want to write are not very aware that it is a state of mind. Most people when they cannot write say, "I can't write. I'm blocked." And then at another point they are writing a lot and they cannot stop; it appears to be a very mysterious thing, writing. Sometimes the Muse is speaking and other times it is not. But I think it is possible to put oneself in the right state of mind in the same manner that some people do meditation. There are techniques to arrive at particular states of consciousness. But we artists do not know the techniques. I do not know, either. I learned to do it with *Fefu and Her Friends* with my notes and record. But who knows? Maybe I could have done the play anyway.

I find that when I am not writing, *starting* to write is not just difficult—it is impossible. It is just excruciating. I do not know the reason, for once I get started it is very pleasurable. I can think of nothing more pleasurable than being in the state of creativity. When I am in that state, people call me, say, to go to a party, to do things that are fun, to do the things where usually I would say, "Oh yes! Of course!" And nothing seems as pleasurable as writing.

But then I finish writing, and that state ends. It just seems that I do not want to go back to it. I feel about it the same way I feel about jumping off a bridge. And to keep from writing, I do everything. I sharpen pencils. In the past few days, it has been a constant thing of sitting at a typewriter and saying, "Oh! Let me get my silverware in order!" It seems very important because, when I might need a cup of coffee, the spoons will be all lined up. Incredible. It is incredible. So I go back to the typewriter. I say, "Oh! I need a cup of coffee." And then, "I better go get a pack of cigarettes so I'll have them here." And then there is starching my clothes. That is something I started this summer. It is a very lovely thing. I make my own starch. I have to wash my clothes. I have to let them dry, then starch them. They are hard to iron. I usually do not press my clothes. I just wear them. But now that I am writing, all my jeans are starched and pressed and all my shirts are starched and pressed. Anything is better than writing.

And Frida Looks Back: The Art of Latina/o Queer Heroics

Cherríe L. Moraga

PROLOGUE: NOTES FROM THE FINCA

The other day, I was introduced to a visiting professor in the Department of Drama at the ruling-class university where I teach. She is a kind of Hot Commodity[1] in performance studies these days, I'm told, and I must be told because for the most part I read things other than White Performance Theory as part of my daily literary diet. We three, the hot commodity, the faculty member who introduced us, and I are all dramatists of a sort, making drama or at least writing about those who do. I welcomed Hot Commodity politely, just the right amount of butch pressure in my self-initiated extended handshake. Just the right amount of eye contact, letting this white woman know that I am one of her kind, a colleague not to be confused with those campesina types, who work the campus cafeteria in forest green aprons; those obreras who shy away from the met gaze while they hold the door open for us when our professorial hands are full of Starbucks and pesto-spread sun-dried tomatoes on focaccia sandwiches. I am used to the movidas of Gringolandia down to the subtlest of physical gesture. I can read the code. Judith Butler might be amused by how consciously I "perform" my role as "club member."

So, Hot Commodity inquires graciously about my work. "Working on a new play?"

Since I do not know what plays she considers "old," I (como pendeja) answer honestly, "Not really. I've been working on other projects. Fiction, mostly."

Never ever admit genre transgression to a gringo theater person. To do so always induces some kind of dramatic display of disappointment, or more honestly, disapproval. Since white people for the most part have the luxury to focus exclusively on one genre where they find ample room for exploration of their concerns, we Latino artists and intellectuals genre-hop constantly, in the effort to conjure a body of work full enough to reflect the complexity of our lives. I am grateful to any writer of any genre or cultura that provides insight, however briefly, into the condition in which we Queer Raza find ourselves.

Reproduced with permission from Robert Bernstein, *Cast Out: Queer Lives in Theater* (Ann Arbor: The University of Michigan Press, 2006), 79–90.

After my thoughtless admission of infidelity to the genre, Hot Commodity adds, "Well, *I* want your plays." And I was reminded of how often I hear that phrase from gringo theater artists—until the time comes to produce those coveted plays. That is what I told the high-profile academic, that as much as I love writing plays, without a venue, one is discouraged from continuing in the genre. I instantly regretted giving her even this much information. It is an embarrassment to admit to one's "peers" that one's work is not sought after. It is an embarrassment to admit it to my students. It is an embarrassment not to have something "up and running" on the stage of some coastal city in this country, including the coasts of the Great Lakes, unless of course you are passionately engaged with a play-in-progress, which has been commissioned by one of those coastal cities.

"Well, they should at least produce your work here," she says. "I'll talk to the chair about it." And then I realize I must've momentarily lapsed in my usually seamless performance as colored, but still thoroughly club, member. She's been at this ruling-class university for several weeks, I, for several years; but *she's* going to talk to the chair about producing my plays. ("Ay, gracias, ladee. Chu weel reely talk to the *patrón* for me? See if chu could get me into la casa grande de la hacienda?") Because she *can*, because she feels her words matter. Because she knows nothing of the institutionalized indifference of the majority of my department to Chicana/o drama or to cultivating a body of Chicana/o actors who could perform in those dramas. Because she doesn't have to know and I do. Peers we ain't.

I debated with myself over the question of including this anecdote. It's easy to tell to a group of Latino teatristas, who laugh out of self-recognition. It is more difficult to put into print and stand by.[2] As well intended as my colleague may have been, her words reified for me the absolute second-class citizenship we Latinos experience in the Amerikan academic and theater communities. From the subtlest of insensitivities to bald racism, the U.S. Latino artist is viewed by the majority art and academic world as a token visitor at best and at worst, an ungrateful obrera. At times I struggle with such analogies, knowing full well the privileged position we hold in comparison to the majority of our Raza, who in fact *are* working the fincas of the landowner and the kitchens of the university. The comparison made here, however, is not among Raza; but between Latino artists and our gringo counterparts. Whether acknowledged or not, we bring a five-hundred-year history of colonization to every act of racism, large and small, we suffer. In short, the colonial model still holds true to our experience.

SLEEPING MY WAY TO THE TOP

The last world premiere of my work took place in 1996. The last world premiere of my work took place as I severed a long-term relationship with a white woman who was the artistic director of the theater company that had premiered the last three major plays of my "career." Those plays had also been commissioned and developed by the Los Angeles Theater Center, South Coast Repertory, Berkeley Repertory, and the Mark Taper Forum, so I am by no means implying that my work, outside of bedroom politics, had no merit in its own right. Nor was my motivation to be with her in any way mercantile. (A meeting of minds, attraction, and shared interest had brought us together.) Still, in the end, it was that white lesbian producer, with whom I shared a bed, who sprang for the eighty thousand bucks it cost to mount an Equity-premiere production in my hometown city. Girlfriend knew how to write some grants. And I credit her with the ability to do so and for the opportunity to realize my work at a production level that showed respect for the work. Professionally speaking, it was an equal exchange of talents. Personally speaking, when I walked out of that relationship, she still had her theater and I my plays. But new plays and playwrights are easily enlisted, whereas theaters that produce Latina lesbian work are not.

I remained plagued by the economics and the sexual-racial politics of making theater in the United States. There's got to be a way to produce Latina lesbian theater without sleeping with the producer or feel like somebody's indentured servant when it does get produced. I don't know how often Latina lesbian theater artists sleep with their producers. Many are solo artists, and since their work requires less expense, they may not have to. Anyway, if the truth be told, we can count the number of out lesbian producers in this country on one hand. So "sleeping one's way to the top" won't get most dykes of *any* color further than a staged reading in a black box behind the live-work condominium of a dot-commer in Gentrificity.

All the latinadyke teatristas I know are funny. Funny on the stage and off, behind the scenes and closed doors, and always out of the closet. Their courage cheers me up. Sometimes. Sometimes, the best of them make me sad as I laugh for what I know they know I know they know but ain't gonna say en voz alta because the white girls won't get it/like it/buy it and, for as shabby as conditions are, white girls are all we got and we gotta make our tortillas and frijoles any way we can cuz we ain't nothing without a stage. I say we ain't nothing off the page without a stage.

I haven't had a premiere of my work in five years; although I believe, one of my strongest works, *The Hungry Woman: A Mexican Medea,* is more than deserving.[3] Since then, my work has grown progressively queerer, full of closeted and out-of-the-closet lesbian murderers, but with heroic aspirations. Maybe that's the problem. I do not condemn my sweet suffering sapphic sadists. I empathize with their condition. Who wants to buy that?

DANGEROUS OFFERINGS

Theater scares me all the time. My words made flesh pain me. Often. Often in my mind I believe I must be able to pay my actors high sums of money to do my work, especially the specifically lesbian work, because what I require of them as women is so damn hard-won. What *is* the compensation?

Still, there was that one time in which I had what the whitestraightboyplaywrights get all the time: an actor who thoroughly reflected my sensibility, who wasn't frightened of it; and one with the skill and talent to embody the character I had envisioned and make it her own. In a staged reading of *The*

Hungry Woman I watched a young Chicana lesbian actor, whom I had invited to perform the role, work for the words in a way I had never witnessed before. This was a Chicana dyke actor playing a Chicana dyke; eager to un-cover areas of her own battle-bruised loving made flesh on the stage. I was not alone and neither was she. We had each other as artists. This was the first time in my life I was not writing and directing in translation, not sexually, not racially. I was working in true and equal collaboration. Her performance would win her my artist's heart and rights to direct and produce the work in Los Angeles a few years later.

Then there was her lover-counterpart in the play, my "leading lady," played by an actor I had for so long wanted to see embody my most mad Medea. She is an actor of great talent. But (how do I speak of this?) how is it intuitively I feel they flee from me, these artists who know better; women who have the intelligence as actors to see the full breadth of a role and yet run from it. Or they appear onstage and walk through it as skilled craftspeople with no soul. Am I completely *loca*?

Directing the play, I tell my lesbian actor, "Grab her like this." I demonstrate (not very directorial of me, I know, but I do not have the time for "process" with less than three hours before the work goes up). I weave my fingertips in one gesture of bravado around the back of the neck and deep into the greñas of my leading lady. I hold her head up to me. It is an "I'm going to fuck you" gesture. She knows it. So does my lesbian actor. But there is something gra-tuitous in the move, I know. Something that wants to tell this straight woman who plays a (sort of) straight woman in love with a lesbian that I, Cherríe Moraga, know what her middle-aged dissatisfaction is all about. This is a play and this is not a play and I know. Still, I feel bad afterwards, as slight as the transgression was, knowing that I crossed a small invisible boundary, know-ing full well she'd been transgressed by plenty of male directors, gringo and Chicano alike. Maybe what bothered me the most is that I cared. I wanted my Medea to know that the play could be hers if she'd stand inside it; but I couldn't consciously show her my ofrenda and have it rejected.

Real lesbian plays are dangerous. Dangerous to their actors, directors, playwrights, as, I imagine, real queer and colored male work can be. I recall how many times playwright Ricardo Bracho has told me of the gay or straight man of color unable to do a role Ricardo has written because it is too intimate. Too damn close up even for queer boys who may fuck men, but for godsake do not look them in the eyes while doing it.

When I was younger, my actors (straight and gay alike) sometimes fell in love with me. This was okay because it provided a kind of additional incen-tive for the long hours of rehearsal and pitifully low pay. It was also okay be-cause it was usually unreciprocated, a passing interest seldom acted upon and one that, I had the good sense to realize, had little to do with me. Now I'm nearly fifty and without the sexual appeal of a thirty-year-old. If some misguided actor does fall in love with me, it remains unexpressed. I imagine my age is intimidation enough or possibly my woman, who towers a good seven inches above me and most of them. But that "falling in love," especially by heterosexual female actors, meant something to me. It was indicative, I believe, of the actor's willingness to take to heart the meaning of the play.

It opened up the *possibility* of lesbianism in her life. It made lesbianism real, unrehearsed, dangerous and compelling. No wonder we have such a hard time casting our plays.

JOURNAL ENTRY AS PERFORMANCE TEXT; OR, HOW I WRITE A PLAY, A POEM, A POLITIC

After reading *Funnyhouse of a Negro* by Adrienne Kennedy on Martin Luther King Day, 2001.

You know I uh gave up theater you know when you know my language escaped me you know I uh threw a party and nobody came you know I was so damn tired a my own trapped words but once released you know they were uh taken away not the way I intended. And uh cuz a that, you know those prisonwords set free I have made enemies a the best of friends. I am uh starting you know to show you know like the cracks in my consciousness and skin. I am uh starting to repeat myself, stutter, hesitate in front a crowds a more than a hundred. I am, you know, like losing it friends n fame n fortune cuz uh one day I uh you know my prisonwords escaped me.

"If I had a penny for every time you said 'you know' I'd be a rich woman."—Sister Mary Something, Immaculate Heart College, 1971.

I went on 'ster to become a public speaker and be paid great sums of money for what I know. Now my speech is covered with you knows because I know they don't get what it is I'm digging at so I just keep self-affirming, you know, you know, you know . . . cuz I'm scared all the time of what's worse they don't because they won't.

Digging. Sister-playwright Suzan Lori Parks digging up them holes of history in her plays. They think she a freak still she keep on digging probably dig for the rest of her time here: I think that is a life well spent. Finding the hole between the "you" and the "know" and having the plain guts to pick up a shovel.

"I know you are a nigger of torment." That's what Adrienne Kennedy writes. I write, Carajo! When is a Mexican gonna write something that bold and blue? When? When we gonna get mad enough? But no, we left here still commiserating with our cousin Cortez. Ya. Lo. Sabes.

THE BODY FAITHFUL

Some time ago, I went to see Sweet Honey in the Rock perform. They are an a capella ensemble of African American women who have been performing together for over twenty-five years. I first saw Sweet Honey in 1977 in a women-only San Francisco cafe called the Artemis Society. It packed in a crowd of about fifty women. In 2001, Sweet Honey was playing to crowds of thousands in the Zellerbach Auditorium on UC Berkeley campus.

For reasons I don't remember now, I was a little broken-hearted when I went to see Sweet Honey that frozen January night. Maybe that accounts for how easily their voices entered me and brought me to contemplative pause, momentary as it was, in my life. That's something that only art can do: wake you up to remembering something of what you value in your life, something of what you've been missing for too long.

Their performance gave testimony to the power of the female colored spirit, moving freely with legs open and a shared voice wide enough to inhabit the ancestors that paid them visit. And I tried to understand why art is so undervalued in this country: why profit-making and academic pursuits and politics are more important than the expression of the deep soul that inspires collectivism and wards off the suicide of isolation. They sang freedom songs that made me want some for all of us. Of course, I understand how art has been taken from us. Of course I understand that commodified art keeps us for sale, which is exactly where Corporate America wants its colored artists. Of course, I have the analysis. But I wonder why we are not hungrier for an art of our own making? Why do we, ourselves, require so little of our art? Watching those women move on stage, I witnessed, for a brief moment, the once-freedom of the African female body. Has U.S. Latino work achieved even a hint of this yet, this clambering toward freedom? Has our work even approached the *naming* of that loss—lo indio y lo africano—inside the myriad formations in which it takes insistent residence in us? Do we imagine our Native and Black bodies are reconciled, buried beneath the cloak (or is it yoke?) of our perfectly blended "Latinidad"?

My continued faith in the revolutionary potential in colored queerness is the requirement of its physicality, its faithfulness to the body. As we politicized our desire, we politicized our right to a freedom mandated by the body. Our art wants to follow accordingly: to respond to the body's messages in all its racial and sexual silences and contradictions. In that lie our fear and our own self-censorship. In that lie the further marginalization of our work and the confrontation with our own diablitos of fact and fiction, including our self-doubts about our worth as artists. But, as Guillermo Gomez-Peña tell us, out there in the margins is where the vanguard is finally found for those who care to stop, pull their sinking barquito out of the mainstream, and swim on over naked to the far (and darker) side of the river.

THE FAR SIDE OF THE RIVER

I am not alone in this place. Hélène Cixous writes: "Writing and reading are not separate, reading is a part of writing. A real reader is a writer. A real reader is already on the way to writing." I consider how much reading matters to me, how in my literary travels I collect images and ideas and authors and artists and imagine them allies in my jornada. I think of the queer Latino writers who have moved me in some way and I know that it has something to do with heroism, some place of risk-taking, a small truth told without apology.

I remember experiencing this heroism watching Marga Gómez, a veterana stand-up comedienne, take the dangerous leap into performance art in the dramatic chronicling of her mother's illness in "Memory Tricks." I witnessed queer heroics in the sexual nationalism of first-time playwright Ricardo Bracho's *The Sweetest Hangover*. Neither white man nor naked ass appeared onstage, but

Bracho insisted it was still queer. Two years later, in his second play, *Fed Up: A Cannibal's Own Story,* Bracho would stage another affront to the white male hegemony of American theater when his young colored queer "cannibals" eat the remains of the Dead White Writer:

CANNIBAL PLAYER: I liked the taste of his hand. The crunch of the delicate finger bones. . . . Did he fist you?
CANNIBAL HUSTLER: No. Did you fist him?
CANNIBAL PLAYER: Yes. You know I did. . . . He had a terrible smell. Inside and out. . . . Did you eat his ass?
CANNIBAL HUSTLER: No just his heart.

These are moments of queer heroism, dramatic moments, sometimes neither gay nor straight, but always queer hungry. José to Camen in *The Have-Little* by Migdalia Cruz:

I wanned to put my ten fingers inside you. I wanned to feel up inside you till I had my hands around your heart. I could always feel your heart down there Carmen. I wanned to touch your heart.

And there are those moments of the ridiculous, which only the queer mind can conjure. Pingalito in Carmelita Tropicana's *Milk of Amnesia:*

My favorite expression when you want to find out the color of someone you say: "Oyeme mano ¿y dónde está tu abuela?" . . . which brings us to fact three. Three-fourths of all Cubans are white of Spanish descent and a lot of these three-fourths have a very dark suntan all year round. When they ask me: "Pingalito, and where is your grandmother?" I say mulata y a mucha honra. Black and proud.

Macho confessions. Truths told. Secrets stripped naked by the queer eye of the beholder. Jaime Cortez from *Virgins, Guerrillas & Locas:*

Through Amador, I know something of masculinity. . . . The delicate filigree structure . . . splinters at the slightest strain. One wrong move, voice modulation, or clothing choice shatters the brittle machista architecture, and the fuck-up is left standing amid the rubble, vulnerable as a pomegranate in mid-November with its skin ruptured open, tender jewels exposed. (180)

A risk taken: to say what we see. A generation before Jaime Cortez, Arturo Islas broke taboo and exposed the "tender (family) jewels" of Chicano masculinity in his 1984 novel, *The Rain God.*

Felix loved . . . when the sky, charged with lighting, became fresh with the fragrance of the mesquite, greasewood and vitex trees. . . . When Felix was a child he would run outside and dance when the storm clouds passed over, while his brothers and sisters hid under the bed. Neither Mama Chona, nor later his own family, could stop him.

"You'll be struck by lightning," they said.
"Good. I'll die dancing."

We learn later that a young serviceman he picks up in a bar beats Felix, the closeted homosexual of the novel, to death. He, in effect, does die dancing in the effort to express his sexuality, as Arturo would die of AIDS several years after the publication of *The Rain God*. What will encourage us to continue to write what is taboo when the risks seem so high? Where do we get support to do so? Is it that we are still afraid to "die dancing?"

I must confess, in recent years, I feel censored by queer relatives more strongly than blood ties. Possibly because my blood ties (the ones that truly matter) have already proven their unshakeable loyalty not based on the words I've written, but the life I've lived (even with all its fuck-ups of which there have been plenty). Recently, my partner and I attended the opening of a Latino queer art exhibit in San Jose. The invitation we received in the mail held a disclaimer warning that the material in the exhibit might not be suitable for children. We hesitated. Should we bring the kids?

Linda responds, "They only write that because it's gay."

"You think?" I say, imagining the disapproving glances of other guests, as our seven- and eleven-year-old gaze upon erect six-foot high acrylic penises. I regretted later that we didn't take the kids when, true to Linda's hunches, the exhibit displayed ideas and images our children witness everyday of their lives. Just queer. The most natural thing in the world. Linda was right. It was the queerness itself that warranted the disclaimer. It is the "making public" of queerness (that is, its politicization) that makes queerness taboo within our community, not the sexuality itself.

Driving back from SanJo that night, I tell Linda that I see that's what makes some of my comadres so nervous, so frightened. Many of the women I love the most are not "out" in their lives. Sure, everyone knows they are dykes, after twenty-five years or more in "the life." But as much as some of these women have politicized their Chicanismo, their latinidad, even their Indianism, their sexuality remains unspoken, without politicization. It is openly accepted by being openly ignored. I have never, except once, tried to make home with these semicloseted lesbians; made love, yes, but never home. Because home is lesbian. Thoroughly. Still I continue to love these women from my deepest places. And yes, they are family; in the way only Latinos seem to make all Raza familia. As such, the betrayals between us are most palpably experienced, stronger than anything any white woman could do to break our hearts. They push me out there, my queer closeted comadres. They say, "Go 'head, Cherríe, you say it for us." Until I see I'm out there left holding the pussy in public all by myself.

Maybe this anthology is really just a gathering of all those queer artists and writers who, like me, are left (metaphorically speaking) holding the pussy in public. The stage is empty, you're ready to do your number, you turn around, and the backup girls have vanished. You know the backup girls, the ones you just went partying with at the gay bar the night before. You know the one whose hand you held when her woman dumped her for the last time. You know the cousin de corazón you'd kick anyone's ass for hurting. They gone. It's just you up there alone on stage, holding the pussy all by yourself. "Go 'head, carnala," they whisper from wings. "You say it for us."

And you do. You speak. You say it for them and for all of us.

There are moments of rupture such as these, ruptures of queer heroism, in art. Brief flashes of image, word, sound that respond finally to that most censored desire. When we witness them, we are breathless at the self-recognition. We wonder how we have gone for so long without this mirror of our most intimate self.

EPILOGUE: FREEZE FRAME

Chavela Vargas, at eighty-three, sings to Frida Kahlo, in the figure of Salma Hayek. Hayek sits across a cantina table from the aging lesbian singer, whom the real Frida knew intimately more than half century before. It is a Hollywood movie. But for a moment, I forget Hollywood and think only of México, México and its mythic memory. Chavela sings the classic song "La Llorona," the Weeping Woman. And in the split second between frames, Chavela appears as the living Llorona, her face, la calavera. She is La Muerte, Death: our greatest fear and strongest ally, as all free women are.

When the camera settles upon her, Chavela takes on the shape of each of our Indian grandmothers: the sad eyes and expressive mouth. But there is something else at work here for those of us who know Chavela as an uncompromising lover of women. Chavela's age is testimony to our history and to our survival as out lesbianas. She is that site of our most coveted and dangerous freedom. Chavela sings to Frida, her eyes fixed on the Hayek's face. "Me quitarán de querete, llorona, pero de olvidarte nunca . . ."[4] And Frida, unafraid, looks back.

NOTES

1. I refer to my visiting colleague as such to illustrate how the academy, like the capitalist economic system in which it operates, places value based on what is being bought and sold on the intellectual market.

2. The professor to whom I refer is Peggy Phelan. After sharing the essay with her, she requested that I acknowledge her by name in print. "It'd be more honest," she said. As I do not feel my critique of Peggy is particular to her, but emblematic of institutional racism, I chose instead to name her in this endnote.

3. *The Hungry Woman: A Mexican Medea* was finally produced in the fall 2002, directed by Chicana Lesbian, Adelina Anthony, who also played a lead role. Coproduced by Celebration Theater of West Hollywood, Anthony's production company, My Lucha, single-handedly saw to the full realization of the play.

4. Translation: "They might stop me from loving you, weeping woman, but I will never forget you."

Conversations with Ilan Stavans

Esmeralda Santiago

Esmeralda Santiago (Puerto Rico, b. 1948) is the author of *When I Was Puerto Rican* (1993), *América's Dreams* (1996), *Almost a Woman* (1998), and *The Turkish Lover* (2004). With Joie Davidow, she has coedited two anthologies of Latino literature: *Las Christmas* (1998) and *Las Mamis* (2000). This interview took place in Boston, Massachusetts, April 2002.

IS: Why is *When I Was Puerto Rican* in the past tense? Have you ceased to be Puerto Rican?

ES: By no means. The title is meant to be a statement of my experience as a Puerto Rican in the United States. The first thing that happened to me here, about a day after I arrived, was that I met a young girl who spoke Spanish, and we just began chatting as girls will do, and she said that I was not Puerto Rican—I was Hispanic or Latina. She said, "When we're here, if you're Puerto Rican, you're Hispanic; if you're Cuban, you're Hispanic; if you're Mexican you're Hispanic." It was a shock to me that just by coming over from Puerto Rico to Brooklyn I had ceased being who I was. The title is a comment on this labeling that happens to us the minute we arrive here. It's the beginning of a process of questioning our identity. I don't think it's necessarily one of losing it but of thinking about it in a way that we aren't used to.

IS: What is the process that involves you in the actual shaping of a memoir? Is there also a present and past tense between how you lived your life and then when you start writing, how you look at it as a past experience, as an adventure?

ES: It's an interesting thing as a memoir writer, because your life is your work. For me when I begin to write a book, when I decide that what I'm

First published in: Stavans, Ilan. *Conversations with Ilan Stavans* (La Plaza), pp. 194–201. University of Arizona Press, 2005. The first inverview aired on PBS-WGBH on September 16, 2002. Courtesy of Ilan Stavans.

going to write is memoir, the first step is thinking about what the voice is like, because the voice is what speaks to me of what the experience that I'm going to be relating is. By its nature you cannot write everything that happened to you. It would be dull, not to mention painful. So for me it's a question of finding the right tone from the beginning and making decisions about what it's going to sound like. And then the process of choice is actually one of editing. I write as much as I can possibly remember and just keep at it until I feel like I've reached the point where I have to stop. This is usually around the five-hundred-page mark. Then I begin to select what scenes will remain, what events aren't necessarily important in this book, and structure the book that way through the process of elimination and editing.

IS: Talk about self-censorship. When one writes a memoir, certain events, anecdotes that might be too painful for oneself or perhaps, and even more important, too painful for the family to know that they will appear on the page and that other people will find out . . . Are you conscious of certain things that perhaps shouldn't be known?

ES: It's not that my life is an open book or that everything about me is worth knowing or is known, but when I write the first draft, I try to be completely free and nothing is off-limits. I will write about anything, the most embarrassing, the most painful, the funniest, whatever, and the choice comes at the editing stage. At that point I decide what this is going to be, what are the major themes that have emerged in all this writing that I've allowed to flow freely.

IS: Have you had any experience of somebody, a mother, a sister, a friend that tells you, I'm not happy with that part that you tell?

ES: I've been incredibly fortunate in the response that my family has had to my books. They have been generous and, I must say, mature in the way that they read the books. I think that even more sometimes than the readers themselves, they realize that I'm writing about a time that has passed; I'm writing about who we were. My mother will be the first to say, "That's the way things were, things are not like that now." So they have this attitude of, I'm writing about the people that they were, and it reflects on the people they have become. They're proud of this work actually. They thank me. They feel like they are a part of it. I'm writing about them, and so they claim part of the process for themselves and have been nothing but complimentary and supportive all along.

IS: Your books fall into the tradition of the immigrant story, in your particular case Puerto Rico. You were born in the city but lived the first thirteen years of your life in the countryside and eventually moved to Brooklyn and started a new life. They tell us about the American dream. Who is your audience? Is it an audience made of immigrants? Are you writing for a core American audience so that that audience sees what the Latino or Puerto Rican experience is about? Are you conscious of all this?

ES: I've no desire to even imagine who's going to read my work, because that would stop me from writing. If I start imagining people reading what ends up being intimate moments in my life, I don't think I would ever sit down to write. I write for myself, and that's how my writing began, in my journals and my diaries. It was a way for me to understand what was happening to me in this country. And it's ironic that my story is thought of as an immigrant story because as Puerto Ricans, born American citizens, we are not immigrants, we're migrants. We are the same as somebody from Texas moving to Alabama. There's this irony about it and also this tension in what I'm writing because most people who aren't aware of the special relationship between Puerto Rico and the United States have formed opinions about who we are without knowing who we are. I think of my books as documents to help them understand. But I don't get to that point until I'm actually in front of an audience and look out and see who's reading and buying them.

IS: How is your book perceived in Puerto Rico? Latino authors, and Puerto Rican authors on the mainland in particular, complain that their books are not read, even acknowledged at times, in their places of origin. But your particular case is an exception. You are extremely popular in the island. You're recognized, you're a celebrity, your books have been adopted in the school curriculum. They are in libraries. But there is a reaction of a segment of the readership that says, Well, you're presenting a stereotypical portrait of the Puerto Rican, an unpleasant one, one that isn't for us—single motherhood with many children, poverty, the projects, etc.

ES: I'm a stereotype . . . I'm the child of a woman who ended up being a single mother with many children on welfare living in roach-infested tenements in Brooklyn. This is the reality. I'm not making it up, and I'm not going to pretend otherwise or in any way whitewash that to satisfy people's idea of what a Puerto Rican should be depicted like. That's up to the people who had a different life. They should write their own books, and I encourage that and want to see that because I think it's important. But as a memoir writer, I would be doing a disservice not only to myself, to my memory, to my family, but to other Puerto Ricans who share this experience by pretending that it's prettier than it was or cleaner than it was or anything other than what it was. I do feel like it's my responsibility to be as truthful and honest as I can about it. And then people will just have to arrive at their own conclusions. At the same time, that is what has made these books popular. I'm writing about real people. A stereotype is a flat picture of a person. You only see whatever you want to see: it's defined and narrowed. What I've taken is that stereotype and tried to humanize it. And tried to bring the human aspect of these people to readers that recognize themselves and hopefully will learn something about themselves. To people who have a problem with my depiction of the stereotype, the only thing I can say is, You will have to encourage and support other writers to come up with other stories, because I'm writing my truth, and I can't pretend that I had a convertible when I was sixteen. I mean, that's just not the way my life was.

IS: Is it possible to live without stereotypes?

ES: People need shorthands to get to know one another or to see each other. Unfortunately, the problem with stereotypes is that they're a negative way of knowing people. It's not a positive way. If we think of a positive way, we would call it an image. But the other side of that is, yes, I'm a stereotype, I write about having been a stereotype, but this is a stereotype who went to Harvard, who lives in a suburb, who lives a life that is not at all like the life I lived before. I've managed to go beyond that, and that is part of what my books do for people, as I understand it from the mail that I get. It allows them to see themselves reflected: I'm a single mother . . . , or I'm the child of a single parent . . . , or I live in these conditions . . . It is indeed the stereotype of Puerto Ricans, but somebody has risen above them, somebody is overcoming them. It's not what I'm presenting per se in my work but the fact that it's being presented and humanized and expanded upon. It gives people a sense of their own humanity. A stereotype takes away your humanity, but a work of art brings that humanity and makes it real, expands you, and that's why people are responding to it in a positive way.

IS: In order to go beyond the stereotype, education played a major role in your life. As you describe it in *When I Was Puerto Rican* and *Almost a Woman,* you had crucial teachers, role models that encouraged you to pursue certain talents, to explore certain areas of yourself that would open up new possibilities. You went to an important performing arts school in New York, and eventually to Harvard to a writing program. On the other hand, often as minorities we see education as a period when we get away from our roots. We're told we're different, we're told we're tokens. Talk about the process of going through these educational institutions and how they changed your identity.

ES: I had to learn to be strong. The hardest battle that I fought as a human being, especially in my early adolescence, in those first few years that I was in the United States, was to disbelieve the stereotype, to consciously refuse to accept prejudice, racism, classism. I just had to consciously make that decision and say, This teacher may think that I'm not college material, but I will prove him wrong. Or this teacher may discourage me from wanting to study medicine, but that's too bad for him, you know.

IS: It won't stop you . . .

ES: I wasn't willing to let other people define me. That's a part of my personality. I don't know where that came from, and I can't take any credit for it, but I do think that's what allowed me to do the things that I did and allowed me to focus. Every time somebody would throw me just the tiniest little piece of rope, I would grab it, and when they didn't, I just looked for the next person who was going to throw me a little piece of rope. It was a question of taking the opportunities that I saw and going with them in a conscious and focused way and refusing, just absolutely refusing, to believe that I couldn't do the things that I wanted to do. I refused to believe it was impossible, and it didn't matter to me who told me that I couldn't do these things, because they were not me.

IS: One of the ubiquitous elements in *When I Was Puerto Rican* is your tenacity, the perseverance in spite of all odds or against all odds, the finding out that you've a path in which words are your tools. Your way into the world and your way in the world of words. What about your discovery of literature, the first readings that you made, the first writers. How did you decide to become one?

ES: My first introduction to literature was with my father, who's a poet and who loved poetry and would recite the greats of his generation. I was also fortunate to have received my elementary education up to the seventh grade in Puerto Rico, where literature and poetry were an important part of the curriculum. We were required to memorize a poem a week and recited it in front of the whole class. Most of us recited pretty much the same things to one another. The schools were poor, they didn't have great libraries, but they had the works of the greats. To hear Cervantes read aloud by somebody was not foreign in my tiny rural schools in Macún, Puerto Rico. That was something that just happened every week. When I came to the United States and I discovered the public library and I could borrow the books and bring them home, it was like a whole world opened up. I understood, yes, we lived in a tenement, we're on welfare, there're eleven people in three rooms, we don't have much, but I can open any book and learn about another world that is outside of this particular area. And that gave me courage. Knowing that other worlds existed allowed me to dream, and to be tenacious and to be persistent and to refuse to believe the negative stereotypes. So literature for me is not just something I do on the beach; it's something that I live. I lived the books that I read; I lived their lessons. I truly believe that reading saved my life. For other people, it can and will save your life if you're willing to believe it can. There are other worlds and possibilities for you.

IS: Reading and writing saved your life. What did it feel like when you first saw a book of yours in one of those libraries like the temple that you're describing?

ES: It's indescribable. As a writer, when you walk into a library, you say to yourself, Why would I even attempt to do this when there are already so many books out there? But as a reader I knew that there were no books about my experience, because I was at that library every day. There were no books about Puerto Rican girls living in Brooklyn struggling with language, a single mother, lots of sisters and brothers having dreams that people kept trying to squelch. There were no books about that. I remember my local library featured *When I Was Puerto Rican* prominently because I'm active in this library, and I was so proud of myself, because I said: a child is going to walk into this library and see this book and maybe he or she will feel less invisible in this society.

IS: Like you did . . .

ES: Yes, like I did. And see that book and he or she will find something in themselves that will allow them to become the person that they can be, and that is the best thing I could possibly imagine.

IS: With time you have become a spokesperson for libraries nationwide. You're also the author of a novel, *America's Dream*. What's the difference between writing novels and writing memoirs? Is the writer freer with fiction?

ES: No, I don't think it's that easy. It lies in the question of responsibility.

IS: Tell me.

ES: When I'm writing memoir, there are people who are alive. The only image that other people are going to have of these people is what's in the pages of this book. So I've a responsibility to be fair to those people I love and even to people I cannot stand. I have to be fair to them because it would be unfair to show my side of it because I'm the writer. I'm aware in the editing process when I'm selecting the memories that will be included in a memoir of the responsibility I have to those people.

IS: Responsibility means balance.

ES: A balance, but also I have to humanize them. It would be easy to turn your memoir into a way of getting even with all the awful people who ran through your life or all the boyfriends who you didn't like. That is easy to do. It's much, much harder to make those people human, and that's what I strive to do even with the people who are not quite so nice to me. I want to bring their humanity forward. Writing is too hard, too precious, too important.

IS: In fiction . . .

ES: In fiction you have the same responsibilities, but you're writing about yourself. All those characters are me. It was Flaubert who said, I am Madame Bovary. Well, I am América González. But I'm also Correa. I'm all my characters, and so the responsibility is to the truth within myself. And to try and be true to the ugly feelings as well as the feelings that are much more pleasant to hear about.

IS: You recently adapted *Almost a Woman* into a PBS movie for *Masterpiece Theatre*. Was it painful?

ES: It was difficult, because the second memoir, *Almost a Woman*, was much harder for me to write than *When I Was Puerto Rican*. I had forgotten, had wanted to forget, that part of my life. To write a memoir and then to relive it by writing the screenplay and selecting the scenes that would be the most interesting to watch, as opposed to what you write in a book, which has different goals, was a difficult process. Then to see it being filmed and see people who looked like me and my family portraying those scenes was painful, because I had to live those moments again, and I had to make sure that the portrayal was true to the people who first experienced them. It was a difficult process, one that allowed me to understand more about the power of words and the power of experience and how you can take an experience that seems so simple. The film is about how Esmeralda comes to New York, goes to school, graduates from high school. That's all it is . . . But between the beginning and the end there's a lifetime of experience that I share with millions and millions of people, not only Latinos, but people from all over, men as well as women. I remember sitting in a room surrounded by friends the night that the film was broadcast, realizing that 18 million people are looking at this, and saying to myself, This is the most terrifying moment of my life. I was glad that I was surrounded by friends and family, because it would have been too lonely a moment without them to support me.

IS: Could it have started the other way around, a screenplay that becomes a memoir?

ES: Well, I couldn't have written that. I don't think that I could have made those choices. I don't think that I would have made the same choices for the film.

IS: It isn't your medium, either.

ES: No, it isn't. Screenplay writers would hate me for saying this, but I don't think of scripts as a literary form. I think of them as blueprints for whole casts of talented, creative people to present their vision in a medium that they know well. For me, writing this screenplay was a frustrating experience for that reason. The first thing I had to lose was all my favorite cousins and aunts and uncles that didn't make it into the film.

IS: All that family.

ES: It just didn't fit the theme of the film. And there's also the budget and other considerations I don't have when I'm sitting all by myself in my room ready to write my stories.

Selected Bibliography

Anzaldúa, Gloria. *Borderlands = La Frontera: The New Mestiza*. San Francisco: Spinsters/ Aunt Lute Foundation, 1987.

Anzaldúa, Gloria, ed. *Making Face, Making Soul = Haciendo caras: Creative and Critical Perspectives by Feminists of Color*. San Francisco: Aunt Lute, 1990.

Arrizón, Alicia. *Latina Performance: Traversing the Stage*. Bloomington: Indiana University Press, 1999.

Arrizón, Alicia. *Queering Mestizaje: Transculturation and Performance*. Ann Arbor: University of Michigan Press, 2006.

Bernstein, Robin, ed. *Cast Out: Queer Lives in Theater*. Ann Arbor: University of Michigan Press, 2006.

Caminero-Santangelo, Marta. *On Latinidad: U.S. Latino Literature and the Construction of Ethnicity*. Gainesville: University Press of Florida, 2007.

Delgado, Richard, with Jean Stefancic, eds. *The Latino/a Condition: A Critical Reader*. New York: New York University Press, 1998.

Fahery, Felicia Lynne. *The Will to Heal: Psychological Recovery in the Novels of Latina Writers*. Albuquerque: University of New Mexico Press, 2007.

Foucault, Michel. *The History of Sexuality, Volume 1: An Introduction,* trans. Robert Hurley. New York: Vintage, 1990.

Kevane, Bridget, with Juanita Heredia, eds. *Latina Self-Portraits: Interviews with Contemporary Women Writers*. Albuquerque: University of New Mexico Press, 2000.

Mirabal, Nancy Raquel, with Agustin Laó-Montes, ed. *Technofuturos: Critical Interventions in Latina/o Studies*. Lanham, Md.: Lexington Books, 2007.

Moraga, Cherrie, with Gloria Anzaldúa, eds. *The Bridge Called My Back: Writings by Radical Women of Color*. Watertown, Mass.: Persephone Press, 1981.

Postlewate, Marisa Herrera. *How and Why I Write: Redefining Hispanic Women's Writing and Experience*. New York: Peter Lang, 2003.

Ruíz, Vicki, eds. *Latinas in the United States: A Historical Encyclopedia*. Bloomington: Indiana University Press, 2006.

Ruíz, Vicki, with Virginia Sánchez Korrol, eds. *Latina Legacies: Identity, Biography, and Community*. New York: Oxford University Press, 2005.

Sandín, Lyn Di Iorio. *Killing Spanish: Essays on Ambivalent U.S. Latino/a Identity*. New York: Palgrave Macmillan, 2004.

Scott, Renée Sum, with Arleen Chiclana y González, eds. *Unveiling the Body in Hispanic Women's Literature: From 19th Century Spain to 21st Century United States.* Lewiston, N.Y.: Edwin Mellen, 2006.

Torres, Lourdes, with Inmaculada Pertusa, eds. *Tortilleras: Hispanic and U.S. Latina Lesbian Expression.* Philadelphia: Tempe University Press, 2003.

Trigo, Benigno. *Remembering Maternal Bodies: Melancholy in Latina and Latin American Women's Writing.* New York: Palgrave Macmillan, 2006.

Index

About the Editor
and Contributors

EDITOR

Ilan Stavans is Lewis-Sebring Professor of Latin American and Latino Culture and Five College Fortieth Anniversary Professor at Amherst College. He is the author, among other books, of *The Hispanic Condition* (1995), *The Riddle of Cantinflas* (1998), *On Borrowed Words* (2001), *Spanglish: The Making of a New American Language* (2003), *The Disappearance* (2006), and *Love and Language* (2007); editor of *Growing Up Latino* (1993, with Harold Augenbraum), *The Oxford Book of Latin American Essays* (1997), *The Poetry of Pablo Neruda* (2003), *Encyclopedia Latina* (2005), *Lengua Fresca* (2006, with Harold Augenbraum), and *César Chávez: An Organizer's Tale* (2008).

CONTRIBUTORS

Ian Barnard is assistant professor in the department of English at California State University at Northridge. He is the author of *Queer Race: Cultural Interventions in the Racial Politics of Queer Theory* (2004).

Debra A. Castillo is Stephen H. Weiss Presidential Fellow, Emerson Hinchliff Professor of Hispanic Studies, and Professor of Romance Studies and Comparative Literature at Cornell University. She is the author of *Easy Women: Gender in Modern Mexican Fiction* (1998) and *Re-dreaming America: Toward a Bilingual Understanding of American Literature* (2004).

María Irene Fornés is a playwright and director. Her works include *Promenade* (1965), *Fefu and Her Friends* (1977), *The Conduct of Life* (1986), and *Letters from Cuba* (2000).

Phillipa Kafka is Professor Emerita at Kean University and the former director of its Women's Studies Program. She is the author of *The Great White Way: African-American Women Writers and American Success Mythology* (1993), *"Saddling LaGringa": Gatekeeping in Contemporary Latina Writers* (2000), and editor of *Lost on the Map of the World: Jewish-American Women's Quest for Home, 1890–Present* (2001).

Cherríe L. Moraga is Artist-in-Residence at Stanford University. She is co-editor of *This Bridge Called My Back: Writings by Radical Women of Color* (1983); and author of *Waiting in the Wings* (1997), *Loving in the War Years* (2000), and *Watsonville/A Circle in the Dirt: Watsonville: Some Place Not Here and a Circle in the Dirt: El Pueblo de East Palo Alto* (2002).

Esmeralda Santiago is a novelist, memorist, and editor. Author of *When I Was Puerto Rican* (1993), *América's Dreams* (1996), *Almost a Woman* (1998), and *The Turkish Lover* (2004). Editor, with Joie Davidow, of *Las Christmas* (1998) and *Las Mamis* (2000).

Renee H. Shea is professor of English and modern languages at Bowie State University. She is the author of *Marcia Myers, Twenty Years: Paintings & Works on Paper, 1982–2002* (2003) and *"New Frontiers in Fiction," Poets & Writers* (2007).

Jacqueline Stefanko is assistant director of education and training at the American Film Institute.

Sherezada "Chiqui" Vicioso is a poet and essayist. She is the author of eighteen books, including *Algo que decir: Ensayos sabre literatura femenina, 1981–1991* [*Something to Declare: Essays on Women's Literature*] (1992).

Jacqueline Zeff is professor of English at the University of Michigan at Flint.